BOOKS BY
JOHN C. BENNETT

Christian Ethics and Social Policy
Christian Realism
Christianity and Our World
Social Salvation

Christian Ethics and Social Policy

THE RICHARD LECTURES
IN
THE UNIVERSITY OF VIRGINIA

Christian Ethics
and
Social Policy

By

JOHN C. BENNETT

New York
CHARLES SCRIBNER'S SONS
1946

TO

Elizabeth, John, and William

PREFACE

This volume is an expansion of the Richard Lectures at the University of Virginia for 1945. I am grateful to the faculty of the University of Virginia, especially to Dr. Atcheson L. Hench and Dr. S. Vernon McCasland, for the stimulus created by the invitation to deliver these lectures and for their kind hospitality during my visit in Charlottesville. Chapter I is an addition to the original lectures, and I have divided my first lecture into two chapters, II and III. The title of the lectures as delivered was "Christian Ethics and Public Life." The present title of the book was chosen in preference to that because it seemed more accurate.

It is my hope that no one will read either Chapter II or Chapter III apart from Chapter IV. I have used those earlier chapters to emphasize the nature of the problem. While I do not suggest in the later chapters that we have a comprehensive social policy which we can call Christian, I have tried to show that there is essential Christian guidance in the choice of policies and that Christian faith, Christian ethics, and the Christian Church, regarded here as inseparable, are the very stuff of life for the Christian who tries to find his way in society.

I desire to express my special gratitude to my friend and associate, Roger L. Shinn, who has read the manuscript and proofs and has prepared the index. He has made many helpful suggestions and in my absence from the country at the time of publication has helped to see the book through the press.

JOHN C. BENNETT

Union Theological Seminary
New York City
September 1, 1946

CONTENTS

CHAPTER I

The Christian Social Imperative

WITHIN less than a century there has developed a new attitude toward the structure of the social order in most branches of the Christian Church. It was not new for the Church to be concerned about the institutions of society. During most of its history it has been an important factor in the ordering of western civilization. But this modern tendency does have several characteristics which, at least in emphasis and in the way they are combined, are new. This tendency in American Protestantism has taken the form of what is usually called "The Social Gospel," but in somewhat different forms it is to be found elsewhere in Protestantism—especially in Britain—and in Roman Catholicism. The greatest ecclesiastical representative of this tendency in non-Roman Christendom was Archbishop William Temple. During recent years, especially where the resistance movements have been strong, this same tendency has become influential in Protestantism on the European continent. It has been a controlling influence in the great ecumenical conferences, especially Stockholm (1925) and Oxford (1937), Jerusalem (1928) and Madras (1938).

There are three characteristics of this pervasive tendency that make it different from the conception of social respon-

I

sibility that has prevailed in the Church in other periods. The first is only a matter of relative emphasis. It is the extent to which the attitude of Christians toward social institutions and toward social and political decisions is regarded as important. The second is the expectation of large scale revolutionary change in society and the consequent realization that no existing social structure is so secure that we can say that it was ordained by God. The third is the attempt to see the world from the point of view of oppressed or neglected classes and races. I do not claim that any one of these attitudes or convictions has dominated the life of the Church as a whole in any country, least of all the third. My only claim is that where we have the influence of this general social movement in the Churches we do find these three attitudes or convictions operative. There has always been some kind of Christian social imperative, but today these are the terms in which this imperative is understood.

There is much discussion about the present status of the Social Gospel. Is it now outmoded as the result of recent theological criticism? This is largely a verbal matter. This basic social trend in the Churches, far from being outmoded, has gained strength from the early days of the Social Gospel until now. It may be helpful to recognize that the Social Gospel is just the American Protestant form of a much more widespread tendency of thought and life.[1] There are advan-

---

[1] It would be defensible to say that the Social Gospel was the American Protestant form of this tendency from about 1865 until 1930, with its greatest influence falling within the first third of this century. The reason for putting the matter this way is that the Social Gospel was not merely this modern understanding of the Christian social imperative, but that it appeared in the context of theological assumptions that were vulnerable and that are now dated.

tages in keeping the term, Social Gospel, because to discard it might mean a loss of that vital sense of the social imperative that the Social Gospel means for everyone. I shall say more later about the theological context of the Social Gospel that needs to be criticized, but now I shall deal with each of these three characteristics to which I have pointed as the new elements in the modern social movement in most of the Churches.

1. The first of these characteristics is the relative emphasis upon Christian social responsibility. Wherever modern social Christianity has had influence it is taken for granted that the attitude of the Church to the problems of social justice and international order is one essential test of its health as a Christian Church. No degree of depth in theology and no degree of warmth in piety can compensate for failure in social sensitivity.

One of the reasons for this new emphasis is that in the modern period we have so much knowledge of the extent to which a person is conditioned by society. The soul is not an independent entity that has its own freedom quite apart from the body and the environment. The soul is not fully determined by external conditions and it does have the chance to gain an important degree of freedom, but during the most formative years of the child's life these environmental conditions do determine in large measure the growth of the child's personality. During those early years undernourishment, bad housing, the sting that comes from belonging to an oppressed race, the sufferings and dislocations of war, the discouragements that come to a family through unemployment, the effort of a tyrannical state to capture the souls of the young—these external factors are of such great importance that the Church cannot be true to its central mission without seeking to correct the conditions that thwart and distort the growing child. Responsibility for families, for children, is the point where we see the Christian and the Church forced to emphasize the changing of institutions. No longer can we assume that the Christian family is a dependable oasis in any kind of society. In a totalitarian nation the family cannot count on being able to protect the children against corruption by the state. What war does to a family can hardly be imagined by those who have never known their nation to be a battlefield.

Archbishop Temple saw with great clarity the degree to which the individual soul is moulded by social conditions. He put special emphasis upon the effect of unemployment. Unemployment had a more profound effect upon the conscience of Britain than on the conscience of America, perhaps because in Britain there were depressed areas where, before the recent war, unemployment seemed to constitute an almost hopeless problem, and these areas were very close to everyone in a small country. Temple did not feel that the worst evil was the poverty or want resulting from unemployment, for unless the whole country is impoverished these can be alleviated by social services, though he realized that such alleviation has in the past been inadequate. The most serious effect of long continued unemployment is that it means that men are not wanted. "This," Temple says, "is the thing that has power to corrupt the soul of any man not already far advanced in saintliness." Temple explains this by saying: "Because the man has no opportunity of service, he is turned in upon himself and becomes, according to his temperament, a contented loafer or an embittered self-seeker." [2] This is the moral danger of a chronic condition of unemployment.

Another major reason for this emphasis upon social institutions is that today our decisions in regard to them are obviously fateful. In other generations it was always possible to drift, with the expectation that there would be a considerable margin of safety. Drifting would be hard on the millions who have always been the victims of oppressive institutions, but they would not soon become worse off than they had always been and they had learned to be patient. As for the comfortable classes, they had no reason to expect that they would drift to complete catastrophe. But today the interdependence of the world prevents the isolation of any catastrophe. There is an end to the patience of the people who have long endured oppression, and their revolutions, which have great creative possibilities, can take a form that would destroy the good as well as the evil in our civilization. Modern weapons of warfare give a kind of finality to other threats and reduce the margin of safety almost to zero. To see how fateful our social choices are is not in itself a Christian motive for actions. But it is possible for Christians to see in this very fatefulness the wrath of God in the sense that Paul spoke of it in the first chapters of Romans. There is no one of us who does not need to be shaken at times by the sense of urgency that contemporary events force upon us. Otherwise we are always willing to find excuses for postponing steps that we should take, without such pressure, because we see that they represent God's purpose for human life.

2. The second characteristic of modern social Christianity

---

[2] *Christianity and Social Order,* (Penguin) p. 12.

is the acceptance of the fact that radical change of the structure of society is to be expected and that we can no longer be guided by the belief that what has been secure and impressive for generations must be ordained by God. Here it will be possible for our conceptions of the providential working of God to become more harmonious with the revolutionary demand of the Christian ethic. During the periods in which the Church was most active in guiding civilization, there seemed to be a presumption in favor of the existing hierarchical structure of society. There was no expectation of the possibility of large-scale change, and the existing order had an apparent stability and a degree of impressiveness that gave it a false majesty. Privilege has usually been able to take to itself this false majesty. Paul was partly responsible for the crystallizing of this attitude toward the existing forms of authority. His words in the thirteenth chapter of Romans about obedience to the higher powers as ordained of God have been proof texts for all kinds of social conservatism. Even Calvin, though later Calvinists broke away from this conservatism, provided the same rationalization for accepting tyranny.[3] It has been a very difficult thing for Christians to win the right of revolution on theological grounds. It was won clearly only on soil prepared by Calvinistic and sectarian forms of Christianity. Today in the Church, the right of revolution seems to have been won almost everywhere (except perhaps in the Soviet Union!) Pacifist scruples will still be a factor in discouraging revolutionary violence under all circumstances, but scruples based upon ideas of divine providence will no longer constitute a serious inhibition against revolution or any other radical opposition to existing

[3] *Institutes of the Christian Religion*, IV, 25.

forms of power. The old "legitimate" rulers have largely disappeared. Kings, where they claimed real authority, have been dethroned. With them passed the kind of majesty that could become confused with religious sanctions. It will now be more difficult for those who have power or privilege to convince the victims of injustice or oppression that this power or privilege belongs to the order of God.

To say that revolutionary changes are inevitable is not necessarily to promise a better order. The older respect for the established social hierarchy was at least a safeguard against anarchy. Now that we can no longer count on this conservative spirit there are new opportunities for justice and freedom, and the traditional forms of hypocrisy will no longer disturb us. But the danger of anarchy will be greater, and also the danger that we may see more of the tyrannies created by revolution both on the right and on the left. The individual may have more freedom in a static authoritarian society than in a world in which vast movements with popular support sweep back and forth across his world. As for hypocrisy, the most sanctimonious nonsense about the sacredness of the ancient order is no worse than the modern use of ideas by propagandists to mean the opposite of their real intent. I mention these things to keep what is being said in true perspective. It is more important to emphasize that there are new opportunities for both justice and freedom for the oppressed and the neglected people of the world. The Church has been freed from uncritical support of the social hierarchy in many lands. There is no longer in Christian theology and ethics a strong inhibition against revolutionary change.

3. The third characteristic of modern social Christianity is

the tendency for Christians to try to see the world from the point of view of the classes and races that have been most oppressed or neglected in the past. I have said that this is perhaps least evident of the three characteristics here outlined, but it is common where the Social Gospel and other forms of social Christianity have been influential. This tendency is closely related to the one last mentioned, and together they have great importance in changing the mind of the Church. Together they point away from both a socially conservative interpretation of the working of divine providence and a paternalistic understanding of Christian love.

One illustration of this effort to see the world from the point of view of the exploited classes is the way in which, wherever the social interpretation of Christianity has been accepted, there has been a genuine interest in the Labor Movement. In America this goes back to the last decades of the nineteenth century, but in the twentieth century we have seen this interest institutionalized in the Churches. Even denominations that have every reason to be socially conservative, such as the Presbyterian Church (U. S. A.) and the Protestant Episcopal Church, have shown this concern for Labor. The Federal Council of Churches has taken it for granted and its Industrial Division has been a means of expressing the solidarity of the progressive wing of Protestantism with Labor. It is true that there has been a conflict in the Churches that has been only partly recognized between this pro-Labor attitude on the part of many leaders, and even of official agencies of the Church, and the ingrained bias against Labor in the constituency of those Churches that are strongest in the middle classes or in agricultural communities. But here I am speaking of trends of thought and of leadership rather than of the ideas of the average Churchman. The contemporary interest of the Roman Catholic Church in the Labor Movement in countries that are not still controlled by the feudal past is even more pronounced than is the case with Protestantism. This interest is in part a reflection of some of the same ideas that have had their effect upon Christian social attitudes generally, but it is greatly strengthened by the fact that Catholicism in industrial countries is often the Church of the workers. This is of decisive importance in America.

Now that Labor has power, great but still insecure power, the ethical problem has been changed in some measure. In the past the Churches could assume that it was always safer to be on the side of the under-dog on the principle expressed by Walter Rauschenbusch that "the strong have ample means of defending their just interests and usually enough power left to guard their unjust interests too." [4] Today the Churches will need to be more circumspect in their attitude toward Labor as a power group which is often tempted to be unjust to unorganized workers and to other groups that now more truly represent the under-dog, and which is tempted to put some limited interest above the welfare of the public as a whole. But this support of the Labor Movement on the part of Churches still has moral justification because, among the great organized groups in the world, Labor, in spite of all that can be said in criticism of its present leaders and policies, is the group whose real interests are closest to the general welfare.

Another example of the modern tendency of the Chris-

---

[4] *Christianity and the Social Crisis,* (Macmillan, 1907) p. 361.

tians to try to see the world from the point of view of the more exploited groups is the bad conscience which Christians who belong to the dominant race feel about racial discrimination and racial segregation, about the relations between the imperialistic powers and the colonial peoples. So far in this area the Churches have to their credit chiefly words, but there has been a great and increasing volume of words that are sincere enough to be evidence of the bad conscience of which I speak. Paternalistic defences of white supremacy no longer have any standing at all where social Christianity has been influential.[5]

This new effort to see the world from the point of view of oppressed or neglected classes and races is long overdue and it has not changed the habits of centuries, even habits of thought. But this effort is a very promising factor, and it is in part the result of release from the conservative inhibitions that I have already emphasized in conection with the second characteristic of this modern trend. It is in part the result of the new articulateness of these classes and races themselves. Their capacity to present their case to the world and their political power have been enormously increased. It is doubtful if this generation of Christians would have been any wiser than its predecessors if there had not been this effective pressure from events and from organized

---

[5] In the decade of the 1940's there has been a great increase in the number of pronouncements by Church bodies on racial discrimination. The most representative statement that is also forthright in dealing with the problem of segregation is a report adopted by the Federal Council of Churches at its Columbus meeting in 1946. It includes the following words: "The Federal Council of Churches of Christ in America renounces the pattern of segregation in race relations as unnecessary and undesirable and a violation of the Gospel of love and human brotherhood. Having taken this action the Federal Council requests its constituent communions to do likewise."

movements of protest but, given that pressure, we have had a better chance to understand the radicalism implicit in Biblical teachings. Jesus was no political revolutionary in the modern sense but he had a habit of reversing the order of things that men took for granted. In so many ways he made the first last and the last first. We see this in the way in which he dealt with the respectable and the outcast, with the righteous and the sinners, with the rich and the poor, with the Samaritan and the priest and Levite, with the prodigal son and the elder brother, with the lords of the earth and those who serve, with the ninety and nine and the one lost sheep. This radicalism of the Gospel found very little expression in the life of the great Churches during Christian history though sectarian movements have from time to time embodied it. Today there is a chance that the great Churches may come to see what it means for them. At least this is what the modern Christian social movement has emphasized. On Sundays the worshippers may come to know what the words mean when they sing:

> "He has put down the mighty from their thrones,
>   and exalted those of low degree;
> He has filled the hungry with good things,
>   and the rich he has sent empty away." [6]

Our problem then will be to try to correct the new Phariseeism, the new self-righteousness, the new tendencies toward injustice when the men of low degree become the mighty. And this is no remote problem.

These three modern tendencies are the new elements in

---

[6] Luke 1:52–53, Revised Standard Version.

modern Christianity which must not be lost whatever we may think about the Social Gospel. During the first third of this century they appeared in the context of the conventional theological liberalism of the period. The Social Gospel at that time reflected the optimism of the time concerning human nature and concerning the future of civilization. The wisest Christians in the liberal tradition were sure that, while progress was not inevitable, there was evidence that men were solving their greatest social problems. They assumed that the Kingdom of God would be in large measure a reality in human history and that it could be understood as the fulfillment of social progress already far advanced. A great chasm separates us from the period in which men could face the future with untroubled confidence. Within a generation we have plunged from the highest expectations that men have ever held concerning their future in this world to the darkest forebodings that men have ever held concerning their future in this world. We have seen the face of evil in the sadistic horrors of Buchenwald and the less directly intended but horribly cruel fate of the people of Dresden and Hiroshima. We know that, while we may still hope for a better order, there is now reason to believe that all future progress in civilization will be precarious because of the threat of atomic destruction.

This new awareness of the stubbornness of evil in history, of the depth and persistence of sin in our life, that has been forced upon us by events coincided with new influences in theology that owe much to the stimulus of Karl Barth. These new influences are important for our thought but we should not allow them to become crystallized into a new orthodoxy, certainly not into "Barthianism." They have

brought to the American Churches the materials for a better
understanding of the riches of Biblical faith and of historic
Protestant thought, but these riches should be appropriated
with theological freedom. What they may lead to in theological thinking lies outside the scope of these chapters. I mention these theological influences here because it is plain that
they do call for a revision of much that went with the Social
Gospel in America. But they support rather than undermine
the Christian social imperative as I have presented it. The
perspectives of theological thought which they open up make
even more obvious the falseness of the pretensions of the
rich and the powerful, of races and classes that count themselves superior. Most of the representatives of this theological trend that is often labelled "Neo-orthodox" are themselves radical in the sense of being anti-capitalist in their
understanding of the Christian social imperative.[7] Some of
them have taken an important part in the European resistance movements, and know at first hand that the nature
of the political order is of fateful importance for the development of personal life, for the freedom of the Christian family
and of the Church.

The most harassing change of outlook that is required of
us, both as a result of the experience that we have had in
the past two decades and as a result of recent theological
criticism, is the discovery that it is very difficult to relate the
Christian social imperative to concrete decisions in the political order. There seems to be no direct line from Christian
ethics to guidance that will determine what our next step

---

[7] I refer to such theologians, however they are labelled, as Karl Barth,
Emil Brunner, Reinhold Niebuhr, Nicolas Berdyaev, William Temple,
Paul Tillich.

should be in those areas where the next step seems most important. The reasons for this difficulty and the way in which we should deal with it are the subjects of the following chapters.

CHAPTER II

The Distance Between Christian Ethics and Social Policy

CHRISTIANS who are sensitive to the demands of the Christian ethic of love and who have a sense of responsibility for social policy are caught by a great perplexity. This perplexity is increased by the fact that their sense of public responsibility is itself a requirement of Christian love. The acuteness of the perplexity depends upon the clarity with which they see the full meaning of Christian love and the keenness with which they perceive the moral nature of the role that they must play in the world, as citizens or as soldiers or as politicians or as participants in the economic processes without which they or their neighbors cannot live. On the subjective side the ethic of love involves completeness of self-giving to what we believe to be the purpose of God for us in our situation, and on the objective side the meaning of such love can be seen if we realize that God's purpose includes the real welfare of all of his children. If there were a sure path that we knew to be the one purpose of God at any given moment, it would be difficult for us to walk in it, for there would be required a purity of heart that is strange to us. But our perplexity is that we often do not know what that path is. This fact that we do not know with certainty

what we ought to do may become an excuse for complacent
following of the line of least resistance.

This perplexity is almost as old as the Christian Church.
I say "almost" because in the first century, while the
Church was very small, and while Christians felt no need
of accepting continuing political responsibility, and while
their attention was fixed upon the new order that was soon
to break in upon them from above, there was little reason
to feel this conflict. Problems of personal adjustment with
the pagan world—what to do about meat that had been
offered to idols, for example—were real, but Paul dis-
couraged an attitude of extreme scrupulousness in such
matters. Implicit, however, in Paul's acceptance of the
Roman empire as an instrument of God for maintaining
order, for punishing evil doers, is the whole problem. As
soon as the expectation of the sudden end of history became
dim, and as soon as the Church became strong among those
whose lives were much involved in the institutions of the
world, especially after the changes brought by Constantine
and Theodosius, this perplexity became a central factor in
the lives of thoughtful and sensitive Christians. Out of it
came the monastic movements. Out of it came the theological defense of Christian citizenship which is so important
a part of the work of Augustine.[1] Out of it came the peren-
nial sectarian protest against the compromises of the Church.
Much of Church history is the history of Christian strategies
for dealing with this problem. We inherit the results of

---

[1] The heart of Augustine's discussion of this kind of problem is in
The City of God, especially Book XIX, but I desire to call attention to
several letters that should be much more widely read, especially to one
letter from Augustine to a friend named Marcellinus and two letters to
Count Boniface. In the collection of the letters of Augustine these are
numbered 138, 189 and 220.

those strategies and we must, in the light of those results, choose our own. In the next chapter I shall outline several Christian strategies. Now we shall examine more fully the nature of the problem before us.

Why is it so difficult to find a straight line from Christian ethics to the concrete problems of society? In the case of all human problems it is difficult to live according to the Christian ideal. Personal relations are deeply infected by jealousy and hostility. Psychiatric probing has revealed what a nightmare of repressed hostility there may be below the surface of family life. One's own inner life is never wholly free from motives that the conscience rejects if they are understood, and it seems that the ways in which the soul can give expression to a disguised self-centeredness are endless. Nor can we separate this inner world of private selfishness from the outer world of group conflict. The disorders of the soul have their effect upon the disorders of a continent. But there are factors in the social order which enormously intensify the problem. I shall mention some of them.

1. In public life there is a long unbroken history which provides opportunity for the accumulation of disorders, for the development of encrusted prejudices, vested interests that have the sanction of the fathers, vicious circles of fear, hatred and vindictiveness which the wisest contemporaries do not know how to overcome. Who knows how to break the vicious circles of national hostility, for example, to free the Polish question from the entail of past wrongs? If the stalemate between Britain and India is broken, who knows how to dispel the far older antagonisms between Hindus and Moslems? Who can see a clear way to overcome the consequences in American life of the sins of the slave trade?

Who has any answer to the problem of mutual suspicion between Russia and the West, a problem that has a long history and for which both sides are responsible? These are only a few examples of the cumulative character of social wrong. In most contemporary social decisions we find ourselves forced to act at some point in a vicious circle that has a long history.

2. The decisions of public life involve large mixed communities in which only a minority, and often a very small minority, is guided by Christian standards. The Christian citizen must always act in cooperation with citizens who do not even admit the authority of Christian ethics. If he is a politician, or if in any way he seeks to exercise leadership in the community, he has responsibility to people who recognize no Christian commitment. He may be their representative and as such he has no right to act as he might act if he could consult only Christian consciences. It may be his Christian vocation to be responsible to non-Christian constituents, that is, if we believe that there is a Christian vocation in politics at all. This difficulty is very great but it is well for us not to estimate the situation in terms of labels and avowed commitments. While there are profound conflicts in the world between Christians and those who reject even the ethical goals of Christianity, and while there are serious questions concerning the dependence of Christian ethics upon Christian faith, it remains true that in many nations, not least in our own, there is a general deposit of ethical purpose that has been influenced by Christianity. Professor John Baillie finds evidence of the claim that ours is a Christian civilization in the fact that the conscience of our civilization "is still recognizably Christian, that we

judge other men and nations, and to a less extent allow ourselves to be judged, by norms of conduct which Christianity introduced into the world." [2]

Moreover, so distorted and one-sided has been the grasp of Christians themselves upon their own faith that it is often true that men who reject their faith and who have no part in the Christian Church may stand for social objectives that are essentially just, but which perhaps a majority of Church members oppose. No degree of theological soundness and no religious training or experience can be depended on, of themselves, to overcome the limitations of perspective that are the result of one's position in society. Those who know from experience what it is to be unemployed or to be members of a minority race or to be in other ways the victims of society have insights which are essential for social wisdom.

3. The large scale problems of society are greatly aggravated by the fact that we are constantly dealing with people with whom we have no direct personal relationship. Intimate personal relations have their own difficulties that are the result of the emotional development of the individual whose early life is largely a response to the attitudes of parents and others in the family. I do not say that these difficulties are in their way more or less serious than those that we encounter in dealing with people at a distance. It is enough to insist that there is a vast difference between the two kinds of difficulty and that the latter conditions our decisions in public life. The imagination of any one of us is so limited that it is impossible for us to grasp fully the experience of those whom we have never seen and who are

---

[2] *What is Christian Civilization?*, (Scribners, 1945) pp. 46–47.

in superficial ways quite different from ourselves. This difficulty, in imagining what life is like for millions in China or Russia, or any other part of the world of which we may have no first-hand knowledge, is a natural source of callousness. Bishop Gore once said that love is the capacity to read statistics with compassion. Such love is rare, and where it exists the compassion is seldom more than a stereotyped feeling that soon passes and never spoils one's breakfast. There is necessary protection in this because the burden of the world's sorrow would otherwise crush the soul of any sensitive person, but there is a degree of blindness here that distorts judgment.

In the discussion of the obliteration bombing of enemy cities in the war there was one thing that always haunted me. This was just as true of the large scale bombing of Berlin, Hamburg and Dresden as it was of the final use of atomic bombs on Japan. Even though I could not accept the position of the pacifist critics who rejected all such bombing on absolutistic grounds, I could never dispel the suspicion that if I had been an eyewitness of the effects of the bombing upon hundreds of thousands of people in each case, I would have been forced to say that—whatever arguments might be brought forth—these deeds are so evil, so utterly abhorrent to the conscience of any Christian who really knows in detail their human consequences, that they must be rejected. Since the war ended and the full human effects of this obliteration bombing have become known this suspicion has been confirmed.

4. This limited imagination is often combined with conflicting interests, and when such is the case moral blindness is intensified. To see another group, which is difficult to

understand anyway, through the distortions of group-interest is to see many illusions. There is here a serious complication in that the drive of group interest is important in all strong political movements. Where the interest is justified, it has a constructive role. Anyone who is concerned about justice must ally himself with those movements which have as part of their dynamic the pressure of group interest in those who are at present victims of injustice. This is one valid element in the great emphasis upon the Labor Movement that has been characteristic of the Social Gospel in this country. But it is obvious that even justified group interest is not restrained within the limits set by a concern for justice. There is always a push for gains that exceed any just demands— partly as revenge for past wrongs, partly as defense against future misuse of power by opponents, partly as a natural expression of self-interest.

I am not arguing in favor of a narrowly economic interpretation of history, much less for any idea of man as primarily an economic animal. If there is anything that is clear about human nature it is that its deepest drives are to love and to evoke the love of others, to have a sense of security in the approval of others, to be accepted by whatever is regarded as ultimate in one's view of life. Even in the behavior of nations considerations of power and prestige, ideas of honor that may often be distorted and the love of freedom are all effective, though they become combined with economic interest. There are high levels on which the struggle for justice or for particular visions of the Kingdom of God are the prevailing motives of men. All that I desire to stress here is that frequently the common denominator of motive within a class or nation, and therefore a decisive factor in determining policy, is the pressure of economic interests. If we are engaged in holding advantages that we or our group prize against the claims of others, we become rather blind servants of our own interests. But if we ally ourselves with those who are seeking to push their way up against the dominant or the more respectable forms of social power, we give encouragement to the interests of those who, when they have the opportunity, will claim more than justice. In either case we are involved in the struggle between interests which make social decisions morally difficult. The fact that the former case has usually been worse than the latter should not prevent us from recognizing the moral dangers in both.

5. The limitations of our imaginations and the distortions that arise from conflicting interests are further complicated by the extraordinary resources in the human spirit for cloaking self-interest with idealism. Often this is done sincerely. It is much easier to be deceived when there is a grain of truth in the way in which the ideals are used. Religion and patriotism are perhaps the most frequent sources of this confusion. Nations are incapable of seeing themselves as they are; they always look through a fog compounded of idealism and national pride. The bitterness of class conflict in the modern world has been enormously enhanced by the extent to which the classes have been divided by religion. American idealism has been frequently used to support narrow class interests as in the case of the periodic drives of the employers against Labor Unions. Often this has been done to save the country from Communism and Atheism, to substitute an "American Plan" for "foreign" importations, to protect the "freedom" of the worker, in his help-

lessness, to make his own bargain with the employer without interference by the Union. Now that Labor Unions have come to be accepted by a large part of American industry, it is a somewhat pathetic view of human nature that we get from reading the fulminations of employers in the same industries less than a generation ago. The strange capacity for self-deception in the pursuit of what seems to be one's interest may be more dangerous to social peace than the cynicism of men who have discarded all ideals. On the other hand it is probably true that the preservation of the ideals in distorted forms becomes at some stage an opportunity. The next generation may see through the distortions and recover the ideals.

The relation between large scale social groups is made difficult because the individual member of each group is able to express the more altruistic side of his own nature in his group loyalty, and yet that group loyalty will itself be used for imperialistic or other destructive purposes. This tendency has been writ so large over the history of our own times that it hardly needs specific illustration.

6. A sixth factor which makes public life especially difficult from the moral point of view is that personal responsibility is in many ways diluted. The individual citizen has some responsibility for the policies of his nation but it is shared with so many others that it does not come home to him with full force. The elected leader has responsibility to the citizens who elect him, and he cannot in the nature of the case act according to his personal moral preferences except where issues are clear and where he has some kind of mandate from the people. He can pioneer and go ahead of the conscience of the nation at times, but when he does

so he must choose the occasion carefully, and he has ample excuse most of the time for abiding by the will of the people. So, the electorate which is often ignorant of the facts passes responsibility to the elected politician or statesman and the latter passes responsibility back to the electorate. Sometimes this is evasion, but often there is partial justification, for the elected leader is a trustee chosen to protect the real interests of the people. His best chance to pioneer is to see more deeply than the average citizen into those interests on a long term basis and then lead the people by appealing to both their long term interest and their idealism. It was this method that was used with such marked success by Franklin Roosevelt in his attempt to make the nation aware of its responsibility for the outcome of the war in Europe.

The problem of diluted responsibility is as serious in economic relations as in the policies of the nation. The directors of a corporation are responsible to the stockholders; and the chief interest of the stockholders as stockholders, not necessarily as human beings, is in dividends. The whole momentum of a corporation is on the side of increasing profits and all other interests—the welfare of the workers or of the community at large—are secondary. The stockholders themselves may be Christians—they may even be Churches —but they have only a marginal interest in anything but dividends, and since their holdings are usually divided among many corporations, they cannot follow intelligently in each case policies that have ethical importance. The most that can be expected is that, when a particular corporation becomes notoriously bad in its labor policy or in some other respect, the Christian stockholders may take some action, but usually that action is no more effective than the selling of the stock to someone else who is indifferent to the moral issues at stake. This state of affairs makes moral choices very difficult. It blurs even the most important issues so far as the individual is concerned.

The six factors that we have discussed help us to see why the problems of social life are so difficult for the Christian. These considerations show why it is that often we must deal with a vast accumulation of evil, why our public choices are so often choices between only evil alternatives. Emil Brunner has laid bare the full bitterness of the problem in his statement that there are times when we are *obliged* to do evil. I shall quote a passage from *The Divine Imperative*, which is the greatest book on Christian Ethics written by any Protestant in our time:

> "We never see the real meaning of 'original sin,' we never perceive the depth and universality of evil, or what evil means in the depths common to us all, until we are *obliged* to do something which, in itself, is evil; that is, we do not see this clearly until we are obliged to do something in our official capacity—for the sake of order, and therefore the sake of love—which, apart from our 'office' would be absolutely wrong." (p. 227)

The Christian soldier would be the first to see the truth in this hard statement, but it should be just as clear to the Christian citizen who remained at home but voted to send the soldier to be his representative and his defender in battle. I think that it should also be clear to the Christian pacifist, who must at least leave undone some things that are at the moment necessary to restrain evil and who shares, whether he chooses to do so or not, the collective sin of his society.

The literature of Christian resistance in Europe under the Nazis is full of references to this problem of the lesser evil that at times seems to be commanded. How was it possible to resist without being ready to lie and to kill? This would be more obviously necessary where one had to choose between allowing other individuals to become victims of the Gestapo and defending them by deceit or violence. In one international Christian student group that discussed these problems during the war the compromise involved in deceit seemed to weigh more heavily than that involved in killing.[3] An ecumenical leader who had a good opportunity to study the resistance movements in occupied Europe summarized his impressions in these words:

> "Problems which the ordinary text-books on ethics at most treated as hypothetical limit-cases, have become part of the normal experience of many Christian patriots. The problems of lying and of killing traitors may be given as illustrative examples. Trying to find 'the more excellent way' in inextricable and unprecedented situations of moral conflict, many Christians in these years have rediscovered the profound truth that Christian conduct cannot be equated with an anxious, moralistic perfectionism or an angelic Utopianism, but rather means a lowly, dangerous obedience, trusting in the Divine forgiveness of inevitable sins."

---

[3] See *The Student World,* Fourth Quarter, 1943, pp. 245–249. The best source for this kind of Christian searching of conscience during the years of war and resistance in Europe that I know is this quarterly, which throughout the war period has published articles by European Christians that are notable for their sensitivity and honesty.

Those are hard words for any Christian to accept and it is impossible for Christians to see their meaning unless there has come upon them the realization that in some situations every available alternative is evil, that to refuse to deceive or to use violence in defending others may make one responsible for their becoming the victims of the most cruel atrocities.

The full bitterness of this kind of perplexity has become apparent in connection with the atomic bomb. On the surface it should seem clear enough that the atomic bomb is in all circumstances so destructive in its consequences that the Christian can have nothing to do with its manufacture or use. This consideration has convinced those who were already pacifists that their case is now impregnable. But others are haunted by the thought that if atomic bombs should become spread around the world and if effective international control is not developed, the chief protection for humanity against atomic war will be the realization on the part of each nation that if it lets loose atomic bombs on the cities of another nation, its own cities will probably be destroyed in a few hours. I do not say that this kind of fear is in the long run a reliable protection but it is conceivable that there may be a period in which it will be effective. If a Christian should come to the conclusion that this is so, can he ignore all such consequences and become an absolutist even about the manufacture and use of atomic bombs? Perhaps he can do so, but not without assuming a share of the responsibility for any atomic war that may be encouraged by the policy that he recommends. It is significant that when the Churches of Britain and America appointed two commissions to study the relationship between Christian faith and atomic warfare, neither commission was able to agree on this point.[4]

There is yet another set of complications which must be mentioned before we try to find our way to some solution of the problem. The factors which I have already mentioned are in some way related to the moral decisions of the Christian. They all involve some spiritual blindness or they refer to some objective situation which can be kept under moral judgment. The complications with which I shall now deal are morally neutral. In actual life they never come as neatly separated from moral choices as they do in this analysis, and yet it is important to recognize that they have this distinctive character. There are aspects of most social policies concerning which there is no distinctively Christian guidance. There are at least three such strands in most decisions about which we get no distinctively Christian guidance, if we analyze our situation carefully. First there are the technical issues which call for expert judgment. These involve matters of fact about which exact information is called for. They also involve reasoning within an area which calls for special training. Many questions of method are of this sort. The debate about specific methods of preventing unemployment or the debate concerning international monetary arrangements are illustrations of this kind of issue. Most often when we come to specific legislation we find that the difference between two proposed bills for dealing with a complicated social

---

[4] "Atomic Warfare and the Christian Faith," Report of the Commission on the Relation of the Church to the War in the Light of the Christian Faith, appointed by the Federal Council of Churches. See p. 13. "The Era of Atomic Power," Report of a Commission appointed by the British Council of Churches. See pp. 54–57.

problem, such as health insurance or industrial relations, involve technical issues and that these bills are couched in a jargon with which we cannot deal adequately without special knowledge.

A second kind of issue is one that requires the prediction of how groups of men will behave if a particular policy is followed. This is both a political and a psychological question. Expert knowledge is called for but the experts may know very little that is conclusive. Indeed this kind of difficulty is far more perplexing than the technical issues. Through what political party should one work in America—through an existing party or through some new party? That is the kind of issue. Most of our decisions about foreign policy illustrate what I mean. Who knows what the wisest policy is from the Christian point of view in dealing with the Soviet Union? There are no experts here who can give us much guidance. We may know that it is of the utmost importance that Russia be made to feel secure against a future attack from us, but we do not know how that is to be done. We do not even know how far Marxist dogmas about "Capitalist encirclement" are decisive for the minds of the rulers of Russia. We do not know how to convince Russia that her fears are illusions, for in the past there has been so much ground for them. We do not know how far a policy of resistance to Russia's totalitarianism in eastern Europe will aggravate her fears, nor do we know what prospect there is that if she comes to feel more secure she will become less totalitarian. Statesmen, political scientists and the ordinary citizens can do little more than guess at the answers to these questions. Yet it is on just these answers that our most fateful decisions depend. Nearly every hard problem of foreign policy that we face as a nation—how to prevent Germany from becoming the disease center of Europe, how to make stable the changes of attitude that have already appeared in Japan, how to prevent civil war in China, etc.—raises for us questions of this kind to which there is no clear Christian answer.

A third type of issue is the choice between two or more competing values when we know that both or all are important. The discussion concerning the line to be drawn between various forms of private initiative, or the freedom of the individual and over-all public planning of economic life, is of this kind. In the discussion of the dangers of totalitarianism, of the "road to serfdom" there are involved both clear moral issues and also all of these neutral issues. We have to ask ourselves technical questions about any proposed step in the direction of social planning. We have to ask ourselves questions concerning the effect of such a step upon human behavior. Will it necessarily become the first stage in the development toward totalitarianism or will there be various brakes along the way? If this step is not taken what will happen? Usually that question is ignored by the opponents of all planning. We are here dealing quite obviously with competing values—with two sets of values, both of which have a valid claim upon us, the values of freedom and order, the values of personal responsibility and of social security, the values of freedom and justice—different kinds of freedom as well. Here we can argue endlessly and the issues do not yield themselves to sure Christian judgment.

There is great danger here in failing to recognize that these three kinds of neutral issues can be used to cloud the mind and to prevent action that is opposed because of interests that are at stake. Technical issues make a good smoke-screen to prevent change of any kind. When the Churches in 1919 opposed the twelve-hour day in the steel industry, they were accused by the steel magnates of not knowing the technicalities of steel production, and of not understanding the financial position of the industry, but soon all such arguments were swept away. They were irrelevant beside the effect of the twelve-hour day upon human beings. The steel industry survived in spite of the technical difficulties of the eight-hour day and now no one would think of using that kind of argument to restore the longer hours. Each type of neutral issue needs to be dealt with fairly on its own level, but it is important to prevent any such issue from being an excuse for inaction or a front for some narrow interest.

The difficulties with which we have been dealing have long been recognized in varying degrees, and in the light of one or more of them Christians have developed various strategies in relating Christian ethics to social policy. In the next chapter we shall examine several Christian social strategies.

CHAPTER III

Four Christian Social Strategies

(A) CATHOLIC STRATEGY

FIRST, I shall consider some of the resources of Catholicism, especially Roman Catholicism, in helping Christians to deal with the perplexities which have been outlined. There are three resources that are distinctively Catholic.

There is, most obviously, the Catholic idea of the two levels of the Christian life, the level of the ordinary Christian citizen and the level of the monastic life with its detachment from the conflicts of the world. These two levels are closely interrelated. The prayers and the merits of those who have chosen the religious life in the full sense have consequences for the salvation of the rank and file of believers. The multitudes of the faithful who do the work of the world support the institutions of the Church which make possible the ascetic detachment of the few. This vocational asceticism is different from Protestant attempts at ascetic withdrawal which we shall consider later. It is clearly not a self-sufficient strategy for dealing with the world's political problems and the Church is not tempted to regard it as such. The Church is in the world, very much in the world —its laity and its hierarchy—but it does make this provision for oases within which those who seek a kind of sanctity that the world makes impossible may realize their aspiration. This sanctity may often seem irrelevant to the struggles of the world and to be wholly supernatural and other-worldly, but it also has the positive value of preserving a type of life that at least may remind the world of virtues that it could easily forget. The monastic life has its own moral temptations, and the very fact that it exists by virtue of the compromises of the average Christian citizen, limits its moral significance. Yet this vocational type of asceticism will always have some attraction to Christians who feel that something can be accomplished if they can avoid personal involvement in the particular forms of evil against which they must bear witness. There has developed a type of vocational pacifism among Protestants that in some respects resembles this Catholic form of ascetic withdrawal.

A second Catholic resource of an entirely different character is the assimilation of the ethics of natural law or rational morality into the authoritative teaching of the Church concerning public questions. This means in practice that Catholics—Roman Catholics and also in many cases Anglo-Catholics—have a whole system of social ethics which is regarded as Christian, and which helps them to relate the Christian social imperative to the most tangled problems of the world without in their judgment abandoning Christian ethics for a secular standard of morality.[1] It is possible for

---

[1] There is an influential Anglo-Catholic school of Christian Sociology which publishes in England the journal, *Christendom,* and which is known through the writings of V. A. Demant, Maurice Reckitt, Cyril Hudson and others. T. S. Eliot's *The Idea of a Christian Society* reflects this tendency, as does much of the material published in connection with the Malvern Conference, though the Malvern Report itself shows the more Protestant thought of Archbishop Temple. This Anglo-Catholic group is characterized by the confidence that we do know what the true natural order for economic life is, and by belief in the possibility of a new Christendom. It is not agreed about procedures in detail and it seeks to avoid clerical authoritarianism. It has felt the impact of recent Protestant criticism of its position as can be seen in an article by Demant on Reinhold Niebuhr. (*Theology,* January, 1944).

Catholics to think in terms of Christian states and Christian societies whereas these conceptions can only be held by Protestants with great reservations.

One basic reason for this Catholic view of society is the relatively optimistic conception of human nature that underlies Catholic theology. One finds this in Catholic teaching concerning man before and after the fall. Before the fall man had in addition to his nature as man supernatural gifts. As a result of the fall he lost these special gifts but his essential nature was not deeply corrupted. Man does inherit from Adam original guilt that must be washed away by baptism and even after baptism tendencies to sin remain, but there is not the same dark view of man's natural condition that we have in the theology of the Reformation or of modern theologians who are influenced by it. As a result of this optimism about man the Catholic has great confidence in human reason in theology and ethics. This confidence is made easier by the fact that, whatever may be the weaknesses of human nature, the Church is always at hand to guide and correct, and it is not itself, as the Protestant will insist, in danger of fundamental corruption that may cause it to become a blind leader of the blind. So, the Catholic knows what the natural order of life is. He believes that its restoration is a possibility. He finds guidance in the experience of the mediaeval Church in a civilization that he regards as Christian in contrast to the modern secularized society. I can give only a few illustrations of the way in which the Catholic finds his course illumined for him by the Church's teaching concerning natural law.

Natural law teaching on private property has given a definite direction to Catholic thinking about economic problems. The belief in the importance of private property for the welfare of both the individual and society is shared by most Protestants, and indeed in Protestant circles this belief has often been more unqualified than in the Catholic Church, but the Protestant, unlike the Catholic, has no right to assert this belief as an inevitable conclusion of Christian ethics. Catholic teaching [2] on this subject has made it possible for Catholic moralists to eliminate Communism and Socialism as real possibilities for the Christian. This statement needs to be qualified, as we shall see, but it represents an important truth. Catholic social doctrine can also provide a thorough criticism of Capitalism, both the theoretical Capitalism of the free market and the more monopolistic form of Capitalism. There has developed a distinctively Catholic conception of a distributist economic order that is neither collectivist in the Socialist sense nor individualist. The encyclicals of Popes Leo XIII and Pius XI have given the Catholic a pattern for a Christian economic order based upon the control of the means of production by guilds or orders of producers. The important thing is that when the Catholic speaks of a Christian society, he knows what its economic structure should be. The Protestant on the other hand has no such knowledge. There is a growing body of common conviction among Protestants about the ethical principles that should govern the economic order, but when Protestants discuss methods of economic organization, they find no basis for a consensus.

Another illustration of the application of Catholic ideas

---

[2] Thomas Aquinas, *Summa Theologica,* Part II, Q. 66. See the following encyclicals: Leo XIII, *Rerum Novarum,* 3–12, and Pius XI, *Quadragesimo Anno,* 44–52.

of natural law is the way in which the Church employs the principle of a just war. The Catholic has definite criteria by which it is possible to distinguish a just from an unjust war, and the assumption up till the present has been that just wars are possible. As Ryan and Boland summarize these criteria, a war to be just must:

(a) Have been declared by a legitimate authority.
(b) Have a just and grave cause, proportioned to the evils it brings about.
(c) Only be undertaken after all means of peaceful solution of the conflict have been exhausted without success.
(d) Have serious chances of success.
(e) Be carried out with a right intention.

The authors add: "It is also necessary that moderation should characterize the conducting of hostilities and should keep the demands of the victor within the limits of justice and charity." [3] This official teaching of the Church has eliminated absolute pacifism as an alternative for the Christian conscience though, as I shall explain later, there are grounds suggested by these tests of a just war for declaring not only that any particular war is unjust but also that a future just war is difficult to imagine.

The resources of an ecclesiastically developed natural law become of special importance in the concrete case because the Church is able to relate its ethical teaching authoritatively to particular social choices. The Church is wise in making sparing use of the full authority which it claims on a world scale. But the enormous prestige of the hierarchy

---

[3] J. H. Ryan and F. J. Boland, *Catholic Principles of Politics* (Macmillan, 1943) pp. 254–255.

enables the Church to teach with effective though not absolute authority concerning many issues that arise in the social order. The practical effect of this is that the Church can often take moral responsibility for difficult choices and thus relieve the individual conscience of a burden from which the Protestant knows no escape. This would be true of participation in war, for example, which has in most cases been fully approved by the Church without qualification.

These two Catholic instruments of interpretation—natural law and the authority of the Church—which can relate Christian ethics absolutely to the ambiguities of public life do not in practice work as effectively as my description of the theory would suggest. Certainly it is true that Catholics are better able than Protestants to say what the pattern of a Christian society should be. Also, it is true that the Church can take a strong line, negatively, in rejecting a major social alternative. This is true of Communism, for example, and for many reasons apart from the teaching about property. The exigencies of the Church as an institution may determine for the Catholic the attitude that he should take toward public questions. But, there are serious limitations to all of these factors. The Catholic Church is far less united on great social decisions than they would lead one to expect. Catholic moralists disagree, for example, on the desirability of democracy from a Christian point of view. In the worldwide struggle against Fascism, the Church has been badly split. It has almost seemed that it chose to back all sides in order to have good contacts with the winner. In France, for example, a large part of the hierarchy was collaborationist, but some Bishops were a very strong support for the resistance movements and they were followed by the majority of the lower clergy and the laymen. In several European countries Catholic prelates could descend almost to the Quisling level and Catholic prelates could be prophetic leaders of the resistance movements. The Catholic pattern for the economic order has proved to be sufficiently ambiguous to be given both Fascist and democratic interpretations.[4] The Catholic condemnation of Socialism has been lifted enough in practice so that Catholics are now permitted to belong to Socialist parties such as the British Labor Party, the Cooperative Commonwealth Federation in Canada, and the new Christian Democratic parties on the Continent which have taken over a socialist economic program. Of course none of these parties has made the mistake of making Socialism into a total philosophy of life as Marxist parties have done. In general one can say that the Catholic pattern for the economic order may lose most of its distinctiveness. Pius XI in the encylical from which I have quoted prepared the way for this when he said: "it may well come about that gradually the tenets of mitigated socialism will no longer be different from the program of those who seek to reform human society according to Christian principles. For it is rightly contended that certain forms of property must be reserved to the state, since they carry with them an opportunity of domination too great to be left to private individuals without injury to the community at large,"[5] Even

---

[4] Catholicism has been badly compromised by its tolerance of Fascism, but it is only fair to point out that clerical Fascism, to which we have reason enough to object, is not the same thing as the Fascism that makes the state absolute. Pope Pius XI in his encyclical, *Quadragesimo Anno,* while describing the corporative economic structure which he favored, warned against the state-centered and bureaucratic distortions of it with an obvious reference to Italy in 1931.

[5] *Quadragesimo Anno,* 114.

on questions as hot as the Spanish issue there remains the possibility for minority Catholic voices to speak out. When the Russian claims on Poland were being debated in 1944 the Catholic weekly, *The Commonweal,* dared to print an article which a Catholic priest dared to write (though anonymously) supporting the case of the white Russians against Poland.[6]

In spite of the doctrine of the just war and of the rejection of pacifism by the Church there are Catholics who are deeply harassed by the thought that no future war is likely to be free from excessive violence, especially violence against non-combatants. They see that it is difficult, if not impossible, to conduct war according to the prescribed rules. An article by a Jesuit scholar [7] on "The Morality of Obliteration Bombing," which condemns such bombing as incompatible with the Christian ethic and with the idea of a just war, reveals the kind of perplexities which the Catholic conscience will face in any war, however just the cause, if it becomes atomic war.

So, while there are habits of mind and also theoretical resources for dealing with questions of social policy which distinguish Catholicism from Protestantism, the thoughtful Catholic who is independent enough to be critical of the local or national hierarchy has few decisions made for him.

The Catholic emphasis upon natural law has much to commend it when we contrast it with the theology of Barth, which insists on an absolute chasm between the revealed will of God in the Bible and all forms of morality based upon reason or upon common experience. There is a moral order

---

[6] January 29, 1944.
[7] John C. Ford, S.J., in *Theological Studies,* V, 261–309.

that we know something about apart from Christian faith, even though this knowledge is more likely to be distorted than the Catholic moralist admits. The Christian can make much use of the deposit of the moral wisdom of Plato, Aristotle and the Stoics which is already an important part of the Christian tradition. And he can learn from the moral experience of modern men with or without Christian faith who have seen more clearly and in more concrete terms than the ancients the claims of equal justice and of a universal human community.

The chief criticisms of the Catholic use of natural law is that it is thought of in too static and precise terms and that the application of it to specific circumstances, even when the Church speaks, is never so disinterestedly Christian as is claimed. Not sufficient place is given to the autonomy of technical issues with which every moral question is intertwined, and the degree of moral ambiguity in most Christian decisions concerning social policy is not recognized. The difficulties outlined in the last chapter create a greater problem for the Christian thinker than the Catholic can consistently admit. A Christian state or a Christian civilization even under the best Catholic auspices is more corrupted by the self-interest of the groups that control it, not least if they be priests, than is admitted. The root of the difficulty is that there are two areas of human experience where Catholic theology does not prepare the Catholic to find sin to be pervasive—the life of Reason and the Church—and so he is not sufficiently prepared to correct the aberrations of either. I do not claim that Protestants do this correcting well either but historic Protestant theology should leave them with less excuse.

These are my criticisms of this Catholic strategy when it works, but it should be said, as I have already suggested, that it does not always work and that differences of judgment in the Church may leave the Catholic almost as perplexed as the Protestant. He may have an added perplexity: what to do about a Church that claims such superior wisdom and sanctity and yet shows on all sides the weakness that comes when any human institution is exalted above criticism.

(B) THE STRATEGY OF WITHDRAWAL

A second Christian strategy is the total or partial withdrawal of the individual Christian or a limited Christian group or sect from those aspects of public life which create special problems for the Christian conscience. The ascetic withdrawal associated with Catholic monasticism is made possible by the fact that the Church as an institution does not seek to withdraw from the world. It is linked with a frank acceptance of a double standard for the ordinary citizen or householder and for the religious ascetic who seeks to realize holiness on a level of heroic renunciation. The sectarian withdrawal characteristic of Protestantism has no place for such a double standard as an essential aspect of the Christian life, though sometimes in modern days of religious tolerance a kind of double standard is admitted in practice for those who share the convictions of the sect and those who do not but who are yet regarded by the members of the sect as Christians within the larger ecumenical fellowship. The Anabaptist protest against the participation of Christians as magistrates in public life is an important example of this Protestant withdrawal. The Quaker protest against war and all forms of participation in war is perhaps the best known contemporary example of this strategy. The example of the Quakers is interesting at two points. One is that the withdrawal from public life is definitely selective. They have not felt any necessity to renounce the institutions of Capitalism though they have done a great deal to reform their abuses. They have preserved a strong sense of social responsibility and have developed a positive way of dealing with many social problems, especially with social conflicts. They also feel free to cooperate with the war department to the extent of supervising Public Service Camps for conscientious objectors. The other aspect of much Quaker testimony is the confidence of many Quakers that they have a solution for political problems that the state itself should be persuaded to adopt. The Pennsylvania experiment of a total community organized around Quaker ideals was an illustration of the way in which Quakers have often conceived of their ideals as involving political possibilities and also of the perils of such expectations. There are some Quakers who have rejected this kind of positive political program and who in effect have adopted a purely vocational pacifism, admitting the right of other Christians to do through the state whatever is necessary in the circumstances to overcome oppression or to maintain order. On the whole, however, the Quaker position is linked with an optimistic view of human nature which makes it natural to expect that society at large can be persuaded to live according to Quaker ideals.

One of the most interesting contemporary examples of this Protestant strategy of partial withdrawal is the case of the Mennonites. Their theology is influenced by the main line Reformation doctrines concerning human nature and they are under no illusions concerning what can be expected of society as a whole or of the state. Their ideal is the development of a community that is as self-sufficient and thus as free from compromise with the world as possible. They are a rural people and find that a rural community is a better environment in which to escape the sin of the world than is urban civilization. They are pacifists but they do not expect the state to adopt their pacifist principles. They are conscientious objectors to all participation in war and seem rather well satisfied with the arrangement with the government that enables their young men to substitute useful civilian work under national auspices for military service. This is almost a matter of routine with them and so it does not involve the frustrations which Public Service Camps have brought to other objectors who desired to do something that seemed important and relevant to the world's crisis.

The way in which Mennonite principles work out in practice is illustrated by their arrangements with Labor Unions, especially the United Mine Workers Union. They prefer rural life but some of them have had to make their living in mines and factories. Ideally they should have their own factories where particular compromises could be avoided, and there are Mennonite employers of Labor who are now being urged to develop modern industrial communities.[8] In order to enable their members to work in the mines it is necessary to have an understanding with the Union that is curiously like that with the government in time of war. The Union has a closed shop in the mines and it is necessary for all miners to belong to the Union to keep their jobs.

---

[8] G. F. Hershberger, *War, Peace and Nonresistance,* (Mennonite, 1944) pp. 289–290.

Mennonites reject Labor Unions as instruments of industrial strife. Therefore they negotiate with the Union and receive a special dispensation according to which they do not have to join the Union to keep their jobs. They promise never to oppose the Union. They pay the equivalent of Union dues but the money goes to a benevolent fund and is not used for ordinary Union purposes. This is similar to an arrangement in wartime by which Mennonites in some communities at the time of war bond drives bought special government bonds earmarked for relief work and their purchases were credited to the community's quota in the war bond drive![9]

This is one way in which to solve the moral problems of public life. It calls for a legalistic method of determining the involvement of the Christian in the sin of the world. It calls for a shutting of one's eyes to the way in which the non-participater may benefit from the compromises of others, from Union wage scales, for example, or from protection against an invader. It also involves a neglect of the larger problems of justice and world order. The way in which non-participation in war may contribute to the victory of such an oppressive force as Hitlerism does not seem to suggest itself as a problem. The need of Labor Unions to check the autocracy of the employer, to give the workers bargaining power to secure a more just share of the product of industry than would be granted to them voluntarily, the value of

---

[9] *Ibid.*, pp. 173–174. This book represents the largest Mennonite denomination in America, but its description of the Mennonite position does not fit entirely the second largest Mennonite Church, the General Conference of the Mennonite Church of North America. This body, which has 45,000 members, is less extreme in its conception of Christian withdrawal from the coercive aspects of public life, including Labor Unions, though it adheres to its pacifist convictions. It does not represent as clear a contrast to the Quakers.

Unions in providing a more independent status to the worker—these matters are passed over. The ideal in industry is the development of small Mennonite industries in which Mennonite employers would give fair wages to their employees without pressure from Unions and in which all relations would be brotherly. That would have some positive values but the outcome of it would almost surely be a paternalistic system which would itself embody sins less obvious but not necessarily more desirable than the sins of a Union shop. Apart from that, the goal which is here envisaged completely ignores the condition of the vast majority of American workers. Their struggles for better conditions are left outside the scope of Christian ethics except to receive condemnation.

I have enlarged on this strategy because it is more consistent than the Quaker policies and it illustrates so well the problems inherent in the attempt to relate Christian ethics to social policies. Its solution is based upon an essential pessimism concerning the world and—perhaps as a second best—the acceptance of the necessity of developing islands of Christian holiness in a sea that will always be the scene of violence and injustice. The most serious criticism is that it has nothing effective to say to the vast multitude that must flounder in that sea.

This Mennonite strategy seems to most of us who assume full responsibility for the political order to be dangerously complacent and legalistic. It promises holiness to a limited group at the cost of evasion of one's responsibilities as a member of the larger community. Such holiness is itself illusory, for there is real participation in the sins of the larger community that is overlooked. Christians who withdraw from the world are guilty of sins of omission that involve responsibility for evils not prevented. When these things are said, I believe that there may be situations in which the Mennonite strategy would be the best available for Christians though they should always strive for a better situation in which more possibilities are open. In a totalitarian society that has become involved in a succession of wars which have no positive meaning in them the Christian Church might be driven to some such strategy as a desperate expedient. Probably in such a case it would know only a martyred and underground existence. The Mennonite strategy so far has been the search for an environment of political freedom in which governments recognize the significance of conscience. The fact that such environments and such governments exist might seem to be a refutation of the Mennonite pessimism concerning the social order. The choice between that kind of society and one that is totalitarian and oppressive would seem to be one choice for the political order to which the Christian with Mennonite principles would be bound to make as direct a contribution as possible.

(C) The Identification of Christianity with Particular Social Programs

The third strategy is the identification of Christianity with particular social programs or institutions or movements. Those who follow this strategy fail to take seriously the kind of neutral issues which I have discussed—technical questions, problems involving the prediction of human behavior, and the weighing of two competing values when both have real claims upon us. It is these issues which make it difficult to have Christian solutions that include both goals and methods. Those who follow this strategy are usually unconvinced by the argument that most social policies which involve large mixed groups are morally ambiguous.

This strategy is at times the consequence of Roman Catholic assumptions and methods, though Roman Catholicism as a total religious system will preserve areas of transcendence that will not be permanently lost, no matter how much at a given time and in a particular country the Church may identify itself with a particular cause—perhaps a crusade against Communism, perhaps a corrupt Feudalism.

This third strategy is the constant temptation of liberal Protestantism. It is the line of least resistance among all optimistic and idealistic Christians, among all who become easily convinced that their solution of a complex social problem is the only Christian solution. It may be sufficient to suggest familiar examples of this strategy in order to show how pervasive it is in the modern Church, not least in the American Church.

The identification of Christianity with pacifism as a political program is one example. The pacifism of ascetic withdrawal does not claim that pacifism is in itself a solution of the political problems of order and justice. But the dominant pacifism that developed in Anglo-Saxon countries between the two world wars involved the judgment that a national policy controlled by pacifist ideals is the one sound implementation of Christian ethics in international relations. Much Quaker pacifism is of this sort. The pacifism of the Fellowship of Reconciliation is of this sort. The assumption is that a pacifist policy is the method of getting the best results in the long run, all things considered. This assumption has something to be said for it in view of the consequences of modern war. War that makes no place for discrimination in regard to methods so that obliteration bombing—with or without atomic bombs—seems to be approved by the national conscience of a civilized nation may be so uncontrollable a method that nothing can justify it. Moreover its political results can be so interpreted that they appear to contain the seeds of more wars rather than of world order or of real freedom from oppression. The argument of the political pacifist is strong and it is not strange that many sensitive Christians find in this kind of pacifism the best implementation of the Christian ethic. The important point for our discussion here is that this is not the only Christian position. There are Christian grounds for resisting tyranny and aggression, especially for resisting the extension of tyranny by aggression. The pacifist concentrates on the human cost of war, on the horror of mass slaughter. The non-pacifist puts more emphasis upon the human cost of surrendering to such an overwhelmingly evil form of power as National Socialism. It is not enough to suggest that there would be a third way—a way of non-violent resistance—if only there were more Christians, for this way is not often a real alternative for a nation. Military resistance and surrender in recent years have been the only alternatives open to the nations marked for conquest and enslavement. To be in any way a party to a policy of surrender is to many Christians to be involved in intolerable evil just as to many other Christians to be a party to military resistance is to be involved in intolerable evil. I believe that there is significance in the fact that the vast majority of conscientious and sensitive Christians who had to face this bitter alternative on their own soil believed that it was their duty to resist tyranny by force, while Christian pacifism has flourished most in those lands that were one step removed from the actual threat of occupation by the armies or the secret police of the Nazis. So, it is wrong to identify Christianity with political pacifism.

It is equally wrong to identify Christianity with the prosecution of war. This has been well learned in our time and needs no defense. It was the dominant view within the American Church during the second world war that Christians should avoid the mistake made so generally in the first world war of turning war into a crusade that was blessed by the Church as the cause of God. There were just and indeed holy causes involved in the struggle between the United Nations and the Axis, but the struggle itself had roots in the sin and failure of a whole generation. It was essential to avoid self-righteous fury if the struggle was to lead to any hopeful result. It was generally recognized within the Church that the pacifist conscience represented valid insights which all Christians should respect, and that differences of judgment concerning the war ought not to result in a breach in the fellowship of the Church. Actually pacifists and non-pacifists did succeed in holding together in the Church, and the presence of each group helped to restrain the other group from absolute claims for its position. Professor Bainton, in his study of the history of Christian attitudes toward war, finds that a somewhat fresh attitude emerged during the second world war, an attitude of critical and even penitent participation.[10]

Many American Christians have had the experience of

---

[10] R. H. Bainton, "The Churches and War: Historical Attitudes Toward Christian Participation," *Social Action*, January 15, 1945.

making both of these mistakes within a generation. They first identified Christianity with war and then they identified it with pacifism. Both pacifists and non-pacifists in the second world war seem to have learned much from this experience.

It is a common temptation to identify Christian ethics with a particular program for economic reconstruction. There have been many Christian Socialist movements, for example, which have assumed such a relationship between Christianity and Socialism. These have varied a great deal in emphasis, some of them making absolute claims for Socialism as the only Christian position. There was a group in Britain that called itself "The Christian Left," inspired largely by Professor John Macmurray, which, at least before the recent war, found a partial embodiment of its ideal for society in the Soviet Union. It was easier to believe in a necessary connection between Socialism and Christianity so long as the threat of totalitarianism was not taken seriously. It was easy to assume that Capitalism was the Devil, that collectivism *per se* was good and that if society overcame the evils of Capitalism, we could be confident that freedom would be added to justice and security, and that the major cause of imperialism and war would be destroyed.

In contrast to this simple identification of Christianity and Socialism there is a movement that is called the Fellowship of Socialist Christians which has worked out a view of the relationship between Christianity and Socialism that is circumspect and, as I believe, sound at these points. Its members are convinced that the Socialist criticisms of both individualistic and monopoly Capitalism are essentially correct and that it is their function as Christians to work for the social ownership and control of the chief centers of economic power. They do not claim that this is the only possible position for Christians to take because they recognize the morally neutral factors that enter into judgments on these questions. They stress the positive gains that have been made by the bourgeois democracies even though they reject the assumption that democratic freedom depends upon free enterprise for the business man. They are critical of the utopianism of most leftist movements and reject the idea that Socialism is a final panacea that will solve all human problems.[11]

There are many other social programs with which at one time or another Christians have identified Christian ethics without any significant qualification, from national prohibition to the kind of political democracy that has been developed in America. The difficulties suggested in the previous chapter indicate some of the reasons for rejecting this strategy. But deeper than all of them is the recognition that Christianity transcends every social institution and every program that includes both goals and methods.

(D) THE DOUBLE STANDARD FOR PERSONAL AND PUBLIC LIFE

A fourth strategy that is clearly marked is the opposite of the third. It is based upon the assumption that Christian ethics are so distant from social policy that they are irrelevant to the problems of public life and that there must be two independent moral standards, one for personal relationships,

[11] The organ of this movement is a quarterly, *Christianity and Society*, edited by Reinhold Niebuhr.

for the Church or for the Kingdom of God understood in
either an other-worldly or in a futuristic sense, the other
for the state and the world of nations. This strategy may be
rejected and yet it has great importance for thought because
it always hovers over our decisions as a real possibility. It
may be on the other side of the boundary of our own convictions and yet we may be tempted by this position,
whether or not we realize it, if we do justice to the factors
which make public life the difficult problem for Christian
ethics that I have described. This strategy is consistently defended and followed under the influence of Lutheranism.
It is alien to Catholicism, Calvinism and sectarian conceptions of the Christian life. It would be a mistake to call this
position the Lutheran view because it would be rejected by
many Lutherans. It is not characteristic of Scandinavian
Lutheranism and it would be disowned by a considerable
part of American Lutheranism.[12] It is encouraged by assumptions which are characteristic of Lutheranism, by the
sharp contrast between law and gospel, by the strong sense
of the state as having primarily a negative function as a
dyke against the consequences of sin, and by the tendency
to accept the authority of the state in its own sphere as final.
Theological pessimism about what is possible in public life
combined with a rigorous view of the distinctiveness of the

---

[12] It was significant to find an editorial in *Lutheran Standard* (Decem-
ber 30, 1944) the organ of the American Lutheran Church calling for more
interest in social action. The editorial begins with the words: "Future
Church Historians may discover that the year 1944 was a transitional year
for the Lutheran Church in America, at least in one domain, namely, in a
new awareness of social responsibility." This refers to American Lutheranism in general, but the American Lutheran Church is a particular denomination that is on the whole much more traditional than the United Lutheran Church, and so this editorial is indicative of a general Lutheran trend.

spheres of Church and state make this position seem plausible. There have been accidental historical factors in the case of German Lutheranism which have accentuated the belief in the supremacy of the state and in the divine calling of the nation.

Professor Paul Althaus, an influential German Lutheran theologian, during the recent war stated this position with great clarity. He wrote: "Christianity has neither a political program, nor any inclination to control or censure the political life in the name of Jesus and the Gospels. No Christian law, no Christian standard, exists for the State or for Politics. The order of the Kingdom of God is on a different plane from that of the political order. The latter cannot conform to the former." [13] In developing the standard that should control politics he found himself forced to appeal to the true necessities for existence of the nation. He sought to keep the nation in the fear of God and his thought as a whole avoids a crude tribalism, but what is lacking is any Christian ethical content in the standard that should guide national policy. The most dangerous words in that passage are the words about not censuring political life in the name of Jesus and the Gospels. Whatever may be the difficulty in applying the ethic of Jesus to political life, to withhold Christian criticism of social policy is to open the door to the complete autonomy of a pagan or cynical political ethic.

This position is supported by an overemphasis upon the words of Paul in the thirteenth chapter of Romans, about subjection to the powers that be as ordained of God. It is not difficult to see how a doctrine of divine providence that

---

[13] *Luther in der deutschen Kirche der Gegenwart* (1940), pp. 24–26.

is combined with an unimaginative traditionalism in ethics could lead to a great overemphasis upon the authority of such an impressive existing order as the state, even though the nation-state is a modern development. The inhibition against revolution has been strong in most branches of the Christian Church and the ethics of submission were a useful instrument in the hands of those who exercised power.

This view of the relationship between Christian ethics and public life has received a severe blow in recent years because of the development of the anti-religious totalitarian state. It is helpful to remember that Paul's words about submission and his claim that "rulers are not a terror to good works, but to the evil," that the ruler is a minister of God for good, are not the only New Testament conception of the state. The Roman authorities had been useful to Paul up to the time that he wrote those words, but it was not long before the early Christians saw quite a different side of the Roman empire, and the Apocalypse is a witness to the fact that some of them saw in it a great Beast. Exactly the same development has taken place in our time. German Lutherans who had been taught to regard the state as a minister of God in the public order came to see that the state can become a demonic power that must be resisted. It was hard for them to resist their own government, much harder than it was for Norwegian or Danish Lutherans to resist the occupying authorities which were obviously usurpers, but an important minority of Lutherans in Germany had the insight and the courage to resist their own government. In doing so, they broke with the idea of the moral autonomy of the state. That idea developed at a time when the state was nominally Christian, when the state was the protector and patron of the Church. It was destroyed when the state became avowedly pagan, setting itself up as the absolute, when it was obviously seeking to pervert the Christian religion.

The leadership of Karl Barth did much to free German Lutherans from this morally paralyzing theology. Himself a Reformed theologian, he had seemed in the nineteen-twenties to share this Lutheran indifference to politics though his followers claim that this is a misunderstanding of him. However that may be, he became after 1934 one of the most dynamic spiritual opponents of National Socialism in all of Europe. In a series of books and of open letters to the Christians of several nations, including France, Britain and America, he called for resistance to National Socialism. The Pauline words about obedience to the governing authorities were always on his mind, but he saw that implicit even in that passage was a moral standard by which it was assumed that the authorities would be controlled. "For he [the ruler] is God's servant for your good—he is the servant of God to execute his wrath on the wrongdoer." (Romans 13:4, Revised Standard.) In his Gifford Lectures Barth by implication lashed out against the National Socialist government while discussing this problem of political obedience or disobedience. He said:

> "It could well be that we could obey specific rulers only by being disobedient to God and by being thus in fact disobedient to the political order ordained by God as well. It could well be that we had to do with a Government of liars, murderers and incendiaries, with a Government which wished to usurp the place of God, to

fetter the conscience, to suppress the church and become itself the Church of Antichrist." [14]

In other writings he did not leave any doubt about the implications of such words and he called upon the Christians of Britain to fight with singleness of mind against Nazi Germany on the basis of the same Pauline injunction. This injunction applied to the people of Britain because their government was a just government. It did not apply to the people of Germany because their government was an unjust tyranny. This use of scripture may be a bit tortuous but the results have been sound!

Since the end of the war in Europe we have learned that many of the leaders of Lutheranism in Germany have abandoned this ethical dualism and have come to recognize that it had some part in lowering the resistance of Germany to the moral poison of National Socialism. The Stuttgart Declaration of German Church leaders in October 1945 and the utterances of Martin Niemöller express profound repentance for what Niemöller calls "a mountain of sins and crimes" that appear "after the fog of lying propaganda has dispersed" and reveal, for the future, a new conception of Christian political responsibility.[15]

This development illustrates the extent to which Chris-

---

[14] *The Knowledge of God and the Service of God,* (Scribners, 1939) p. 230. In the course of this struggle Barth developed a "Christological" conception of the state, which means that the state itself is under the lordship of Christ and must be judged by a distinctively Christian standard. This was an emphatic repudiation of the ethical dualism discussed here and it became a weapon for Christian resistance. His little book, *Church and State,* is the clearest statement of this position. It is open to criticism because Barth does not do justice to the kind of difficulties outlined in the previous chapter, and he is in danger of giving a Christian sanction too unreservedly to social policies.

[15] From Niemöller's Sermon in Geneva, in February, 1946, published in *The Christian News-Letter,* March 20, 1946.

tian thought can be influenced by political conditions. In Luther's time the great tyranny was the Church and he emphasized the place of the Christian prince as a protection against this tyranny. In our time the great tyranny has been the totalitarian state and anyone who would be faithful to Luther's spirit rather than to the letter of his teaching could hardly fail to sanction Christian resistance to so evil a power.

This fourth strategy is based upon a profound analysis of the difficulties in relating Christian ethics to social policy; but it is fatal to allow the standards by which the institutions of society are to be judged and the standards which the Christian acknowledges for his own life to fly apart. In the next chapter I shall show how they can be kept together.

CHAPTER IV

The Relevance of Christian Ethics to Social Policy: A Fifth Strategy

WE ARE now ready to face the central question concerning the difference that Christian ethics should make in our choice of a social policy. It may seem to the reader that up to this point the book has been designed to inhibit Christian action! I shall outline a fifth strategy to which I am led by criticism of the four strategies described in the last chapter.

This fifth strategy is not easily labelled, nor is it easily followed. It begins with a complete rejection of the double standard for the Church and state, for personal life and public life. The choices of the Christian as a citizen or as a participant in the economic process are his personal choices. He retains moral responsibility in what he votes for, in what he supports through his part in the development of public opinion, in the policies to which he consents or by which he profits. If he accepts policies which he would not choose to initiate in a world governed by fully Christian standards, he must have reasons for doing that rather than for ultimate resistance even at great sacrifice.

This fifth strategy also rejects the absolute identification of the Christian ethic with the particular policies which the individual believes that he should support. This reserve is an expression of the transcendent character of the Christian ideal which keeps every human program and every human institution under judgment. This reserve is also a consequence of the Christian belief in the universality and persistence of sin. The meaning of this belief in practical terms is that nothing that we do or achieve is likely to be free from distortion by an overemphasis upon those interests that are closest to us or by the narrowness of our own perspective as we make judgments. If we are aware of these tendencies we can in some measure guard against them and correct them, and so they are not to be regarded fatalistically as definite limits to our achievements. But one of the surest ways of being trapped by them is to assume that now at last we have *the* Christian solution. This reserve is also dictated by regard for the elements of what we may call technical autonomy in most social judgments. We can expect that other Christians will differ from us on the methods by which we propose to solve our problems.

To summarize: this fifth strategy is one that emphasizes the relevance together with the transcendence of the Christian ethic and which takes account of the universality and persistence of sin and the elements of technical autonomy in social policies.

I have said that this strategy is difficult to follow. Indeed it is almost impossible to follow it except within a Christian community that is aware of what is involved. Within the Protestant Churches there has in recent years been an impressive development of thought which is consistent with this strategy. The Oxford Conference on Church, Community and State in 1937, one of the great landmarks in the development of social Christianity, charted a course for the Church along the lines that I have just described. Three of the most influential Christian thinkers who have guided the Church in the past decade can be classified best under this strategy though each has his own emphasis—the late Archbishop of Canterbury, William Temple, Reinhold Niebuhr and Emil Brunner. Of the three Temple was closest to the Catholic confidence in the possibility of a distinctively Christian society, and Brunner is closest to the Lutheran dualism, whereas Niebuhr holds a central position that seems an equal distance from both of those tendencies, but the thought of all three is within the limits of the general position which I am describing. Temple was impressed particularly by the technical aspects of social problems concerning which there could be no distinctively Christian guidance. Brunner and Niebuhr give more emphasis to the moral ambiguity of all social decisions. All three show awareness of both factors.[1]

Christian ethics must always be seen against the background of Christian faith. The positive content in the Christian ethical standard is the commandment of love, love that knows no barriers, love that is willing to pay the price of

---

[1] Temple makes clear that on this point he agrees with Niebuhr's thought in his opening address at the Malvern Conference, published in *Malvern 1941—The Life of the Church and the Order of Society* (Longmans, 1941). Professor Brunner has moved much farther away from a dualistic interpretation of Christian ethics in his recent book, *Justice and the Social Order* (Harpers, 1945). Professor Niebuhr is often given very one-sided interpretations by those who judge his thought by one speech or article. His thought represents an extraordinarily delicate balance between the relevance of Christian ethics to action and emphasis upon the transcendence of Christianity and upon the sin of man. It is a dialectical balance according to which the opposing emphases actually support each other. The doctrine of sin becomes a reason for supporting social policies based upon radical criticism of the *status quo*, and the transcendence of Christianity provides a perspective from which these policies are kept under criticism.

the cross. But there is also at the center of the Christian life an attitude of humility before God which is a source of ethical guidance. It is the humility of one who is aware of his weaknesses and sin, who critcizes himself by reference to the commandment of love, who in his hours of worship sees himself under the judgment and mercy of God.

I shall now state five ways in which Christian faith and ethics should guide us in all of our decisions in regard to social policy.

1. *The Christian should be controlled by Christian faith and ethics in the motives that prompt him to make his decisions.* In all life it is difficult to keep such motives from being distorted by pride and self-concern but there is here no necessary difference between private and public life. It is possible for us to be governed by a disinterested and sensitive concern for those on the other side of every social barrier, for those whose welfare is affected by the policies which we support, even though their interests conflict with ours. The difficulties, outlined in the second chapter, that stand in the way of Christian behavior in the relations between large-scale social groups can be transcended so far as the purposes of individual Christians are concerned. They are no excuse for the failure of any one of us who has become aware of their existence. The Church should be an environment in which Christians are prepared to transcend those difficulties.

Christian love that seeks the welfare of all who are affected by any social policy that is supported, that is willing to subordinate all private interests and all narrow group interests to that purpose, is the actual content of obedience to God. To seek to do the will of God in our concrete situation is to seek the good of all of his children. The relation between grateful and faithful love for God and love for all neighbors as motives for action is much discussed in contemporary theology. Fortunately we do not have to decide in most cases which of these is prior to the other because both reinforce each other in our experience. On the other hand there are times of testing when we are dealing with issues that concern the welfare of neighbors whom we have never seen, neighbors in the mass, neighbors who to all appearances lack the human dignity which in faith we assume that all men possess, neighbors who are difficult opponents or enemies. It is in the face of this ultimate test of our love for men that we realize that such love does depend upon faith in God's love for them. But even at that point we find that when this faith is real it is accompanied by compassion, which works directly without the conscious need of religious support, and that in a society influenced by the Hebrew-Christian tradition there are many people who are servants of such compassion without any background of personal religious faith at all. It is doubtful how far such compassion would reach if there were no indirect influence from religious faith. For our purposes it is enough to say that Christian love even in these hard cases is a reality. It can control the motives which drive us to seek the best available social policy.

During the war there was much discussion of the possibility of love for enemies. The main line of public policy was directed to the destruction of the enemy and any one engaged in combat necessarily sought to kill the enemy first. Moreover in combat situations there is no place for the emotions connected with love. Instead there is a complex of emotions including partially suppressed fear that even in the case of a Christian may have the appearance of hate. But it soon passes and it has no necessary connection with hate. The Christian in war regards the destruction of the enemy as a tragic necessity. He may regard it as morally better than surrender but that does not alter its tragic character. He may pray for the time when once more he, if he survives, may deal with those against whom he is fighting as persons, if they survive. He may will the real welfare of the people of the enemy nation and prepare himself to resist all vindictiveness in peace and to work for policies that will enable enemy nations to become equal partners with his own nation in the world community. Any one who has this attitude transcends the temptation to hate, whatever may be his temporary emotions in combat. He will not deceive himself concerning the nature of war, but he will not believe that even in war the command that we love our enemies is abrogated.

There are those who see little value in motives governed by Christian love in the complicated problems of public life and insist on enlightened self-interest as a sufficient incentive. It is true that in the relationship between large scale social groups enlightened self-interest does often seem to fit better what is possible for the majority, and to represent a goal so far beyond present achievements, that it would be foolish to ask for more. Also, the statesman who is responsible for public policy can seldom ask for anything that is in conflict with the long run interests of his own nation, even though he may as a Christian have higher goals. If he does have higher goals he is likely to put his emphasis upon self-interest in his appeal to the public or to the legislature.

In the post-war period the administration in Washington,

in its attempt to get appropriations from Congress for UNNRA or for rehabilitation loans to other countries, has stressed the argument that such action by Congress would be in the interests of America. It is doubtless important to stress national self-interest as a common denominator that would unite a Congressional majority.

It is fortunately true that when a long view is taken there are many points of correspondence between Christian goals and the real welfare of any one nation or group. America's national interest in world prosperity, the industrialist's interest in a general level of high wages, the worker's interest in the solvency of industry, the interest of every nation in preventing a third world war—these are all promising factors in the contemporary world. But there are limits to the effectiveness of the motive of self-interest even in regard to these areas of mutual interest.

It is so hard to keep self-interest enlightened. Unless there is at least a strong body of opinion in a nation that really cares for the welfare of other peoples, the conception of self-interest will slip until it becomes narrow-minded expediency. It is necessary to have those in public office who share this concern.

Moreover, the enlightened self-interest of a whole nation may demand real sacrifice of interests from individuals or groups within it. There is no simple harmony between the interest of each and the interest of all that does not call for real sacrifices of much-prized advantages from many. Any strong man or corporation or nation may gamble on being able to keep more than its share of privilege without endangering the general conditions of welfare too much for its own good.

The existing conflicts of interest between nations and races and classes, even though they could conceivably be resolved in the interests of all, are so deeply rooted that to overcome them would require a passion for justice and fellowship, not merely a discreet balancing of interests. A minority that shares that passion can be a very important factor, much more important than the size of the minority may suggest. Also, the majority are capable of responding to appeals to conscience when issues are made clear. They may not be consistent or sustained in their sensitivity or compassion but they can rise to meet a concrete need. The Gallup Poll in 1945 and again in 1946 showed that seventy per-cent of the American people "would be willing to go back to food rationing in order to send food to people in other countries." [2] The nation as a whole was ahead, not of what the Administration wanted, but of what it believed the people wanted. It was ahead of Congress—not, we may hope, ahead of what the majority of members of Congress wanted as individuals, but of what they dared do under pressure from minorities that were assumed to hold the balance of power in particular constituencies.

So, while enlightened self-interest is a strong support for many policies that the Christian can regard as right, and while it may often be the most that can be relied on as a common denominator of motive in a nation, it needs to be supplemented or at times corrected by a passion for justice, by a vision of true human community, by a real interest in the people of other lands, by dedication to God's purpose for the nations.

2. *The Christian may find guidance in making social*

---

[2] The Gallup Poll for May 14, 1946, *The New York World-Telegram.*

decisions from the self-criticism that is encouraged by Christian humility. If love is the central Christian motive, humility is the major corrective of the distortions of judgment to which all men are prone. Christian teaching about the depth, universality and persistence of sin should prepare us to see the ways in which our own ideas and the ideas of our own nation or social group are influenced by narrow interests and one-sided perspectives. Christian teaching about God's transcending of all human purposes and programs should prepare the Christian to avoid the tendency to make absolute even the best that he plans or achieves.

This aspect of Christian faith should prevent the Christian from regarding any social system, now or in the future, as beyond criticism. It is a curious quirk of the human mind to become easily credulous concerning the ideal character of some social system. This is the baffling aspect of the devotion of many of our most sensitive and high-minded contemporaries to the Soviet Union. Christians are warned by their own faith never to make the kind of claims for any human achievements that are taken for granted by the Communists and their allies. The literature of Communism fosters just such uncritical enthusiasm for a particular social system within history.[3] Whatever may be said for or against Communism as a form of economic organization, and whatever may be said for or against Russian policy at a given juncture, and whatever may be the policy of the Russian government in relation to Christianity and the Church, there will always be a profound difference between the Christian and the Communist ways of looking at life and history so

---

[3] An example of this tendency is Lenin, *State and Revolution* (Vanguard, 1927) especially Chapter 5.

long as Communists make the institutions and policy of the Soviet Union or of any other part of the earth the supreme objects of trust. I shall have other things to say about Communism and about Russia but this must be said first.

In the day by day decisions of the ordinary citizen distortion comes from narrow interest, not his private interest alone so much as the interest of the group in which he moves, which usually corresponds with his private interests. In public opinion polls one discovers this to be true constantly except when some great issue is dramatized, as in the case of the issue between famine abroad and rationing at home. In most of these cases the individual citizen is in a better position intellectually to understand the case of the point of view that is closest to his own interests. He gets this point of view from his associates and from the organs of opinion that have prestige in his own circle. There is usually something to be said for it and this something can be stretched far without any conscious dishonesty. In order to correct this natural tendency it is necessary for a Christian to have more than usual suspicion of any conviction that is in harmony with his own interests. He may be helped by reading journals that have their influence in some other circle than his own.

The habit of seeing one's nation under God, under what we may regard as God's criticism would take most of the poison out of international relations. It would help to break the vicious circle of self-righteous denunciation between Russia and the Anglo-Saxon nations. To be sure our difficulty here is that nothing that we might say or do can be known to the Russian people unless their rulers choose to let them know it. The fact that there cannot be relations of understanding between the people of Russia and the people of the western democracies, and the fact that the people of Russia have no way of criticizing their government on matters of basic policy, create enormous obstacles to good relations. One must admit that the lack of free criticism at home has made Russian self-righteousness abroad hard to endure. But when that has been admitted the Christian in America has a special responsibility for keeping to the fore the realization that though for us there is a Russian problem, for Russia there has been for a long time an American problem. The history of the attempt of the western allies after the last war to destroy Communism in Russia, the bitter years of ostracism broken only by the invasion of Russia by the Germans, the virulent anti-Russian propaganda of America's most widely read periodicals and of the Roman Church which is so influential among us, the fact that we have the atomic bomb and seem to the Russians to hold it as a threat to them because they distrust us on other grounds, the fact that we take for granted our right of control over territory wherever we have a strategic interest from Japan to Iceland, and yet oppose Russia when she claims the same right—these considerations are part of the problem of the peace. They do not of themselves give us the final clue to policy. They do not suggest that we should not be extremely critical of Russia's methods of extending her power in Europe and Asia, particularly the exporting of her ways of dealing with political opponents, but they do mean that we should never allow the people of the western democracies to forget these backgrounds of Russian policy. The memory of them may at some future time contribute to reconciliation between Russia and the West.

The same Christian attitude of humility before God will moderate the vindictiveness of the victorious nations that now have the people of Japan and the people of Germany and her European allies in their power. Outside the Church this needs great emphasis today but within the Church there has already been a great change in our attitude toward the peoples of enemy nations. Christian teaching about the common guilt, about the common sickness of our civilization shared by all nations has helped to prevent self-righteous attitudes toward the enemy wherever it has been taken seriously. Also the very early reconciliation between Christians on both sides of the recent war has been a factor, but this reconciliation was itself made possible by the general recognition that all one-sided ideas of war guilt are mistaken. It has been difficult to combine recognition of the collective responsibility for the catastrophe of our time, with abhorrence of the particular manifestation of evil that we saw in the cruel Nihilism of the Nazis, but this has been done in considerable measure in the Church. The sheer power of military victors is an awesome thing. To see that it is awesome is the beginning of wisdom in the use of it.

In the social conflicts which have become fateful in American life, the first word of Christian guidance must be that Christians begin with their own sins rather than with the sins of their opponents. This will be very difficult. Christian business men will be tempted to stress first of all the sins of organized labor with its new power and aggressiveness and they will be inclined to forget that their own bitter resistance to the Labor Movement in the past, and their own example in acquisitiveness when there were few checks upon them, are the moral background of the contemporary situation. It will also be difficult for Christians in the Labor Movement to make labor self-critical. This is their responsibility. The same thing will be true of the racial conflicts that will become more acute in the near future. The white man may fear and condemn the aggressiveness of the Negro who has gained new political power and has developed an awareness of his rights in a democracy. But the corrective for this is that the white man remember the past, the generations of exploitation and humiliation that the Negro has suffered at the hands of the majority race, and that any power that has come to the Negro is long overdue. The sense of guilt in this situation must be primarily with the white man in the north and in the south. He is in no position to give moral advice to the Negro, but Christians in both races need to be disciplined by the Christian faith and ethic. One of our problems is that no one is in a good position to give moral advice to the groups that have been most victimized— yet they need it.

There is one area in which we can see how humility is needed to correct what has been done in the name of love. I refer to the criticism of Christian paternalism. Genuine and even sacrificial concern for the welfare of others has been expressed in paternalistic forms. The Christian ethic has been given this twist in economic and political relationships from the days of Paul. Paul himself provides some correctives for it but he did not himself see these full implications for the relations between masters and slaves or between men and women. Slavery, industrial tyranny and imperialism have all been defended by sincere Christians because they believed that they could best serve the interests of less privileged people through the use of power over them. The idea that property was a sign of virtue has died hard among those who possessed it. Christian philanthropy has undercut the interest that Christians might be expected to have in raising others to a position of equality with themselves. As suggested in the first chapter, many factors converge in our time to make the case for paternalism less plausible even to the privileged. Social mobility and the articulateness of exploited races and classes have destroyed static ideas of social hierarchy. Anthropological study of groups that were once regarded as inferior has revealed that there are no such inherent differences among large classes of men to justify permanent divisons among them as superior and inferior. In very different ways the American experiment and the Russian experiment have made possible faith in the so-called "common man." But the Christian has one other ground for rejecting paternalistic attitudes toward others— he knows that he cannot himself be trusted with unchecked and uncriticized power over them. Abraham Lincoln saw this truth long before it was generally recognized by the more orthodox spokesmen of the Church when he said: "no man is good enough to govern another without that other's consent." [4]

3. *The third way in which Christians should be guided by Christian ethics in dealing with the most difficult social problems is that everything that they do should be kept under the criticism of Christian love.* Rigorous criticism of existing institutions and rigorous criticism of all proposals for change are both essential. The methods that we use should also be subject to the same criticism. Those who criticize should see themselves within the dilemmas that

---

[4] Speech at Peoria.

confront the statesmen or others who must make some decision in the actual situation. The critic often dwells in a world of alternatives that do not exist for the man who must act in the present moment. The pacifist critic of the nation during these last years of war has seen much that was true but he has seldom allowed his mind to dwell on the human consequences of a policy that would have allowed the Axis powers to dominate Europe and Asia. He saw the evil of war with special clarity but he often did not see with the same clarity the evil of totalitarian tyranny on the march. He saw the human consequences of obliteration bombing and what he said about this may have been right, but he seldom put himself in the position of the man who had the responsibility of deciding between the use of this dreadful method of warfare and what may have seemed to him to be a much longer war. The idealistic criticism of the San Francisco Conference and the United Nations Charter has often been vitiated by the same unwillingness to face rigorously the alternatives.

It remains true that Christian criticism must be applied to what we do with the rigor that the pacifist critic of war employs in a one-sided way. It is probably impossible for the individual Christian to apply this criticism in all directions but the Church can do this and in doing it correct the insights of the individual. Under the influence of the Church the Christian could both support the war and refuse to regard the war as an absolutely righteous war between good men and bad men. He could be reminded that the United Nations were not wholly just. He could call each method of warfare by its right name and at every point refuse to make it appear that evil is good. Necessarily he would find himself in a profound dilemma in dealing with such matters as blockades and obliteration bombing. If he was not a pacifist he could hardly reject these methods absolutely. He would have difficulty in drawing a line between permissible and forbidden methods of warfare, between combatants and non-combatants in total war, or between starving, gassing, burning or bombing masses of victims. But he would find it morally intolerable to draw no line at all. In all cases he would keep the burden of proof on those who claim that the use of such methods will shorten war and that they are, on balance, the lesser evil. This is a slippery slope not only because it is so difficult to find a stopping place in the actual conduct of war but also because it is difficult to prevent a complete loss of moral standards.

What is essential is that we never cease to call any policy by its right name in the light of the Christian standard, that we never attempt to deceive ourselves concerning the real nature of what we do. I have already called attention to some of the differences between Christianity and Communism. Another difference is that, whatever the ultimate ethical aims of Communism may be, its tendency is to justify any means that is deemed necessary without keeping alive a strong sense of moral conflict. Christians in practice have often been guilty of the same thing but their faith, if it is understood, corrects them. The Communist faith even if understood will not correct the Communist at this point. The reason for this difference is that for the Christian every individual person has a status before God which is the source of worth that no political relationship can destroy. When terror is used against political opponents by the

Communists, these opponents have already lost any dignity
that they might have had, in virtue of being opponents of
the Communist purpose or even of the party tactics. To
sacrifice the person who is an opponent is to brush off an
obstacle. It is only the plan, the goal, the collectivity that is
the source of moral obligation. The Kulak, the "wrecker,"
the Fascist (a term now used so broadly that it seems to include all opponents of the Communists) is not a person to be
redeemed but a thing to be removed. Frederick Schumann,
who writes about the Soviet Union with great sympathy,
remarks that the Communists in the famine of 1932 appeared less disturbed by dead Kulaks than by dead cows.
The former were "class enemies." [5]

Arthur Koestler in various writings has posed the ethical
issue that is involved here. He may be too biased an opponent of Communism to be used as an authority on the
Soviet Union in general, but at this point he has analyzed
the problem well, and the fact that Communists do liquidate
their opponents with a clear conscience is not in dispute.
In *Darkness at Noon,* a story of a purge of Communist
leaders in Russia, one of the investigators who is trying to
convince an old Communist that he should follow completely the policy of the government offers this analysis:

> "There are only two conceptions of human ethics, and
> they are at opposite poles. One of them is Christian and
> humane, declares the individual to be sacrosanct, and
> asserts that the rules of arithmetic are to be applied to
> human units. The other starts from the basic principle
> that a collective aim justifies all means, and not only
> allows, but demands, that the individual should in every

[5] *Soviet Politics at Home and Abroad,* (Knopf, 1946) p. 219.

way be subordinated and sacrificed to the community—
which may dispose of it as an experimentation rabbit or
a sacrificial lamb. . . . Whoever is burdened with power
and responsibility finds out on the first occasion that he
has to choose; and he is fatally driven to the second
alternative."[6]

Ever since I first read those words they have haunted me
because it is not only Communist oligarchs and inquisitors
who have chosen the second alternative. Christians who have
given support to the methods of war have also acted in ac-
cordance with the second alternative within a limited context. There are, however, at least two differences between
the Christian who sanctions war and the position that is
here not unfairly associated with the consistent Communist.

The first is that for Christian ethics there is no collective
good that is not embodied in the welfare of concrete individuals. Consequently if individuals are sacrificed as soldiers or as the helpless victims of blockades or bombing, this
can only be justified if we are driven by the evidence to
the conclusion that any alternative policy would lead to the
sacrifice of individual persons on an even greater scale.

Another difference is that at no point will the Christian
cease to regard these means, that are destructive of persons,
as evil. The enormity of this evil will weigh upon him
continually. He will suffer with the victims in this tragic
situation. He will never regard them as mere obstacles to be
removed. He will be driven by this experience to do everything that is possible to create a new order in which such
hateful means will not be required. Doubtless many Communists feel this kind of moral conflict more than many

---

[6] (Macmillan, 1941) p. 157. By permission.

Christians. There have been times when the Church supported persecution of heretics that was similar to this modern terror used against political opponents. In theory, according to the prevailing religious assumptions at the time, such persecution was not inconsistent with the Christian concern for the individual because there was the possibility that it might rescue him from error that would damn his soul; but, where persecution was carried on by the Church to preserve others from the contagion of error, or in the interest of the religious unity of the nation or of ecclesiastical power, it was morally as abhorrent as modern political persecution. Today, while Communism discourages moral sensitivity about means, Christianity creates such sensitivity.[7] Christian ethics without Christian faith cannot prepare us to bear the burden of this conflict between a sensitized conscience and the evil that one may have to do. It would be particularly difficult to allow oneself to criticize what one does with full honesty. The natural tendency would be to slur over the real nature of our decisions and to make them appear better than they are. Complete honesty depends upon faith in the mercy of God who helps men to bear this kind of moral burden. Here, as in other respects, Christian ethics are not self-sufficient. They lead us to a degree of inner tension that may often be too great for the soul unaided by the grace of God.

4. *The Christian ethic guides us in determining the goals which represent the purpose of God for our time.* These are not absolute and all-inclusive goals but the next steps that

---

[7] I need hardly say that my reason for concentrating on the ethics of Communism and for ignoring the ethics of Fascism is that the latter neither in ends nor means has any ethical claim that the Christian needs to take seriously.

our own generation must take. The Kingdom of God in its fullness lies beyond our best achievements in the world but God does have purposes for us that can be realized. To live for them is to live for the Kingdom now. The moral criticism of the means now used makes the search for an order in which better means will be possible all the more imperative.

What are these goals? We can define the nature of them by referring to the idea of "middle axioms." The use of that term in this context goes back to the writings of Dr. J. H. Oldham in preparation for the Oxford Conference in 1937. The term may not be a good one but it points to something that is distinctive and I shall use it for convenience. A "middle axiom" is more concrete than a universal ethical principle and less specific than a program that includes legislation and political strategy. Dr. Oldham says of "middle axioms": "They are an attempt to define the directions in which, in a particular state of society, Christian faith must express itself. They are not binding for all time, but are provisional definitions of the type of behavior required of Christians at a given period and in given circumstances." [8] To agree on these "middle axioms" will still leave many pressing problems unsolved, but clarity about them will give both the Church and the individual Christian a sense of direction. In order to illustrate this idea of the middle axiom I shall suggest middle axioms in four areas.

(A) It is in the discussions of international relations and world order that Christians have come to a wider consensus than in regard to any other major problem. The Commission on a Just and Durable Peace of the Federal Council

---

[8] Visser 't Hooft and J. H. Oldham, *The Church and Its Function in Society,* (Willett-Clark, 1937) p. 210.

of Churches, under the chairmanship of Mr. John Foster Dulles, during the whole period of the second world war has been leading the thought of the Churches on this subject. We may distinguish between three levels of its recommendations. It began with a series of "guiding principles" which represent the religious and moral basis for any political advances toward world order. Here is an example of a guiding principle: "We believe that the principle of cooperation and mutual concern, implicit in the moral order and essential to a just and durable peace, calls for a true community of nations. . . . A world of irresponsible, competing and unrestrained national sovereignties whether acting alone or in alliance or coalition, is a world of international anarchy. It must make place for a higher and more inclusive authority." That is too general to be called a middle axiom but on the next level the recommendation was far more concrete. About two years after the promulgation of the guiding principles the Commission set forth what it called "Political Propositions" (popularly known as "Pillars of Peace"). The first of these is a good example of a middle axiom: "The peace must provide the political framework for a continuing collaboration of the United Nations and, in due course, of neutral and enemy nations." After it was explained that "in due course" meant "as soon as possible" that first political proposition met with very general approval among American Christians. There was a third level of recommendation which was critical but definite support for the San Francisco Charter and the United Nations organization as the only real alternative to isolationism and international anarchy. There were some voices raised in protest against this recommendation because the Charter was regarded as

worse than nothing by those who insisted on world government now or who saw in the Charter only a front for the
hegemony of the great powers. But here again there was a
wide consensus on the ground that at this stage unity among
the great powers was a necessary condition for both peace
and justice, and on the ground that the United Nations organization did include within itself the beginnings of a
more adequate constitutional order among the nations.
Notice the progression—guiding principles about which
there could be no disagreement; a middle axiom which had
behind it a substantial consensus but which related Christian decision to a concrete reality, the United Nations, about
which there could be considerable debate, especially if one
belonged to a neutral or enemy nation; and finally support
of a particular program which was even more ambiguous
and about which there was less agreement. Christians must
move from one to three or to some equivalent of three, but
as they do so the degree of authority that can be claimed in
the name of Christian ethics becomes weaker with each
step.

There is much more guidance from Christian faith and
ethics concerning world order that should be mentioned in
a thorough discussion, especially in connection with our
policy toward defeated enemies and in regard to economic
justice among the nations. We might wish that this guidance
could be more specific than it is even at best but at least it
does mark out a course that avoids both isolationism and
imperialism, America's chief temptations, and that avoids
vindictiveness, the temptation of all victors.

(B) Christian teaching concerning economic institutions
is clear at the stage of guiding principles but among Protes-

tants there is less agreement on this subject than there is about world order. The report of the Oxford Conference provides the most authoritative statement of guiding principles and I cannot do better than quote five principles from that report in somewhat abbreviated form:

(1) Right fellowship between man and man being a condition of man's fellowship with God, every economic arrangement which frustrates or restricts it must be modified.

(2) Regardless of race or class every child and youth must have opportunities of education suitable for the full development of his particular capacities.

(3) Persons disabled from economic activity, whether by sickness, infirmity, or age, should not be economically penalized on account of their disability, but on the contrary should be the object of particular care.

(4) Labour has intrinsic worth, and dignity, as being designed by God for man's welfare. The duty and the right of men to work should therefore alike be emphasized. In the industrial process labour should never be considered as a mere commodity. In their daily work men should be able to recognize and fulfill a Christian vocation. The workingman, whether in field or factory, is entitled to a living wage, wholesome surroundings and a recognized voice in decisions which affect his welfare as a worker.

(5) The resources of the earth, such as the soil and mineral wealth, should be recognized as gifts of God to the whole human race and used with due and balanced consideration for the needs of the present and future generations.[9]

---

[9] The Oxford Conference (Official Report), pp. 99–100.

These principles should be seen against the background of the very drastic criticism of the present economic order in that same report on four counts: that it encourages acquisitiveness, that it creates in some countries "shocking" and in all countries "considerable" inequality, that it is characterized by the concentration of irresponsible economic power and that it very generally frustrates the sense of Christian vocation.[10] At least with these criticisms in mind we can gain some idea of the direction in which Christians would have society move.

Today Christian thinking about economic problems is confused by arguments over free enterprise and social planning. The European Churches have come to accept the trend toward planning as inevitable and as having within it a promise of greater justice. The American Churches are split on this issue. I propose two middle axioms that should be a minimum basis for common action by American Christians:

a. That the national community acting through government in cooperation with industry, labor and agriculture has responsibility to maintain full employment.
b. That the national community should prevent all private centers of economic power from becoming stronger than the government.

Those two goals are illustrations of the sort of thing that can be regarded as necessary in our situation but even to mention them is to raise problems that suggest other goals. For example, while the government must take ultimate re-

---

[10] *Ibid.*, pp. 87–92.

sponsibility to prevent mass unemployment and to prevent any unit of economic power—whether it be a corporation or a labor union—from holding up the community, it is also true that government should be restrained from attempting to absorb all activities. Strong government that can take responsibility when necessary must be combined with the encouragement of non-political centers of initiative and power. There is no universal formula for achieving or preserving this balance. There is no Christian formula for it. This is an example of our constant problem of making our way between opposite dangers. The Christian must have his eye upon both dangers, and he should observe in himself the tendency that is so obvious in others to exploit one or the other danger as a propaganda device, depending on which of them is the more immediate threat to the interests of his own group. There are few people who do not favor government intervention when it is on their side and there are few who do not denounce it as a matter of principle when it goes against them. Some awareness of this situation would make it easier to achieve a balance between governmental and non-political forms of initiative.

(C) The guiding principles that should control race relations are clear enough. The equal dignity of all races before God is generally asserted. The Oxford Conference stated this without ambiguity:

> "The existence of black races, white races, yellow races, is to be accepted gladly and reverently as full of possibilities under God's purpose for the enrichment of human life. And there is no room for any differentiation between the races as to their intrinsic value." [11]

[11] *Ibid.*, p. 60.

This report also laid down a middle axiom about race but it confined this to the Church—the transcending of all segregation within the Christian fellowship. I quote from the report: "In the services of worship, in its more informal fellowship, in its organization and in the hospitality of the Christian home, there can be no place for exclusion or segregation because of race or color." [12] It is right for the Church in dealing with the question of race to begin with itself. It has little that it can say to the world so long as its own institutional life contradicts its essential teaching. It cannot be content, however, and much less can its individual members be content, to ignore the policies of communities and nations. Two middle axioms in this area must come to govern Christian teaching. The first is the securing of equal opportunity for the members of all races in such matters as employment, housing, education, legal protection and political rights. The second is the progressive overcoming of involuntary segregation as a humiliation to the minority race. I realize that there is much sincere disagreement about the relative place of these two goals and also about the time table in working for them but both are morally necessary.

(D) One final example of a goal for public life that I shall cite grows out of the relationship of Christian ethics to democracy. There has been in the mind of the Church no necessary connection between political democracy and Christian ethics in the past. The Catholic Church has had a preference for hierarchical forms of society and even the most recent pronouncements of the Pope can be regarded as ambiguous though they give the impression of support

[12] *Ibid.*, pp. 60–61.

for democracy. The great Protestant denominations did not begin as defenders of democratic institutions though Protestantism prepared the soil in which those institutions have been able to grow. Democracy as we know it in America and in western Europe has two poles. One is popular sovereignty involving majority rule with universal suffrage and the other is constitutional protections for the individual and minorities. The first without the second may lead to totalitarian tyranny with a mass base as we have recently learned through tragic experience. This is the weakness of the Communist conception of "democracy." The second without the first is likely to lead at best to the relatively restrained and decent rule of an oligarchy that is out of touch with the real needs of the people.

Christian ethics do not make this question easy for us for we cannot say that there is any one form of government that is suited to all nations now. Moreover democracy based upon a one-sided optimism concerning human nature, concerning the common man is inconsistent with the dominant strain in Christian teaching about the sin and frailty of all men.

There are, however, good grounds for seeing democracy in the two-fold sense that I have described as a goal toward which Christians should move. First, there is the faith in the potential dignity of all men as children of God, which is as much a part of Christian doctrine as the recognition of the universality of sin. Second, it is clear that constitutional protections for the individual and for minorities are absolutely necessary to prevent tyranny. Third, there is no group that is disinterested enough to have power over others without the check that is provided by universal suffrage.

Reinhold Niebuhr has stated the case for democracy along these lines in an unforgettable epigram: "Man's capacity for justice makes democracy possible; but man's inclination to injustice makes democracy necessary."[13] A cynic could not believe in democracy because for him enforced order would be the chief necessity. One who is uncritical of his own class might be tempted to think that if only people of his type had the power, all would be well. Faith in the possibilities of common men combined with rigorous criticism of human pretensions, especially the pretensions of the respectable and the strong, furnish the Christian basis for belief in democracy. It is significant that Karl Barth, who has always stressed the independence and transcendence of Christianity and the sinfulness of man to the point where the relevance of Christian ethics to social policy is endangered, writes about democracy in the following way: "When I consider the deepest and most central content of the New Testament exhortation, I should say that we are justified, from the point of view of exegesis, in regarding the 'democratic conception of the State' as a justifiable expansion of the thought of the New Testament."[14]

5. *The fifth element in this strategy that I am presenting is the attempt to counteract some of the consequences of what we must do as citizens or in some official capacity by action of another kind.* There is a margin of freedom for Christian action for the individual or for the Church apart from the main line of social policy in which the nation or the community as a whole may be involved. The importance

---

[13] *The Children of Light and the Children of Darkness,* (Scribners, 1944) p. XI.
[14] *Church and State,* (Macmillan, 1939) p. 80.

of this non-official corrective action has been made clear to me by Professor Emil Brunner's discussion of the subject in *The Divine Imperative*. He shows that "we never meet other people merely within the orders," that is within the limits of our official responsibilities. As Brunner says: "the 'office' only constitutes one aspect of life; it is the first point, but not the last, it is the shell which contains life, but not the life itself." And then he adds: "actual life consists in meeting another person in love." [15] This apparent separation of what one does officially from love as the motive is misleading because Brunner rejects a double standard for public and private relationships and regards love as the ultimate motive for what we should do in all spheres of life.

There are two ways in which we find room for this corrective action. One is in face-to-face personal relations. A man does not live and act in only one capacity in relation to others, even in relation to the same people. A man is not just an employer or employee, a soldier or a statesman, a judge or a prosecutor or a policeman, an American citizen or a German citizen. Brunner uses as one of his favorite illustrations the judge who must decide according to the law and not as he might prefer to do in the light of all the extenuating circumstances or of the needs of the concrete case. He says that the judge as a Christian may still allow the accused to know that "in the spirit of solidarity he bears his guilt with him." [16] This may be difficult in practice in many cases but one can see how this represents the ultimate demand of Christian love for one who occupies that position. The same is true of anyone called to discipline another in

---

[15] *The Divine Imperative*, (Macmillan, 1937) pp. 227–8.
[16] *Ibid.*, p. 228.

behalf of an institution, whether he be Dean of a college or Warden of a prison. In time of war the soldier has only a minimum of freedom to deal with the enemy as a person but, if he is a Christian, he is not just a soldier when he meets the enemy as prisoners, as wounded or as non-combatants. When the enemy is defeated the soldier in an occupying army will have innumerable opportunities to be more than a soldier and the ultimate effect of the occupation may depend upon his use of them.

The second way in which we can see how a Christian can counteract in one relationship some of the effects of what he must do in another is the result of his membership in the Church. The fact that I am at the same time both a citizen of a nation and the member of a universal Church is a source of considerable ethical freedom. Even in war, which surrounded us with so many ugly necessities, Christians proved to be free to keep in existence channels of reconciliation that were used as soon as the war ended. In the case of many decisions that limit our action, decisions that mean taking sides for one movement or party against another, membership in the Church furnishes a relationship across the line of conflict that may modify the conflict itself.

At the beginning of this chapter I said that this strategy is not easy to follow. The burden upon the mind and the conscience of the individual Christian is very great for he must finally bring together all of these factors that have been outlined and make his own decision. For the Protestant there is no escape from this burden. Often the decision is an either-or decision with no reservations so far as immediate action is concerned, though there will be reservations in attitude that may influence the quality of the action in some measure and which may affect the possibilities of future action. If the individual Christian were alone, the burden of this responsibility for decision might well become intolerable. As a member of the Church he may find guidance for action and channels for action. In the next chapter we shall consider the distinctive function of the Church in relation to social policy.

CHAPTER V

The Ethical Role of the Church in Society

PROTESTANTS have recently come to see in a fresh way the importance of the Christian Church. This is a return to the emphasis of the Reformers themselves who, in contrast to later Protestant individualism, were profoundly concerned about the Church. There are many reasons for this contemporary interest in the Church but·there is one that has special significance for the attempt to relate Christian ethics to social policy. During the period in which liberal Protestants had most confidence about the developing social order in the world, the Church had a subordinate position, for the real Christian community in which men felt increasingly at home was not the Church but society in the process of being Christianized. A generation ago it could be believed quite readily that nations which had a Christian background were as nations on the point of conforming to the principles of Christian ethics. One of the wisest men in the American Church was able to write in 1912: "The largest and hardest part of the work of Christianizing the social order has been done." [1] Then all that

---

[1] Walter Rauschenbusch, *Christianizing the Social Order*, (Macmillan, 1912) p. 124.

seemed needed were more devoted effort and more patience and a dominantly Christian social order would come soon. Now we live in a world that is appalled by the horrors of the war and of its aftermath, with more baffling problems than our fathers could have imagined, and we are haunted by fears of an even greater catastrophe.

In our time the Christian Church has a function for the Protestant that seemed unimportant in 1912. It is needed as a base for operations in a world that is still alien. It is needed as a source of guidance and power and healing for those who must take up the hardest tasks in the world. It is needed as a bond of union between people who are divided by the most dangerous social and political conflicts. It is needed as a community within the larger community of the nation, a community that for its very existence as a Church must have freedom to speak, a community that owes its allegiance to God who is above every earthly power. It is needed as an ethical laboratory, where it is possible to push further in the realization of Christian goals for human life than can be done in society at large.

The existence of the Christian Church has this ethical meaning for the Christian: he is at the same time a citizen of two communities. As Augustine said of the two cities, the City of God and the City of the World, these communities lie confusedly together.[2] Disciplined by Christian faith in the Church, the Christian citizen will use his best judgment to discover what the next step should be in the nation or in the world. Because he is under the influence of Christian faith he will not claim that the next step is any better than it really is. Moreover he will be encouraged within the

---

[2] *The City of God*, Book XI, Chapter 1.

sphere of the Church to find ways of counteracting the evil in the political choices that he must make. The Christian Church, with all of its shortcomings, is the only school in which we are trained for this dual citizenship. This seems to be the age of the state and it would be a mistake to deny that the state must increase its functions in many directions. It alone has the power, and it alone is in a sufficiently central position to do necessary planning in a complicated technological society. But the more extensive the work of the state becomes, the more important it is to encourage associations within the larger community which are independent of the state. The Church is the one association which has proved over and over again to be so tough that the state cannot absorb it. It becomes for that reason a protection for human freedom, since it is a voice of criticism that continues to sound when most other voices have been silenced.

I am taking for granted here a Protestant view of the Church which stresses the visible community of Christians but which counts the form of the institution that holds the community together a secondary matter. Also I am taking for granted a Protestant view of the Church which insists that at all times the Church should be kept under the criticism of Christ as we know him in the New Testament. A Christian Church should always be open to criticism—both from within and from outside. The greatest danger confronting any Church is that it may come to make itself the measure of what is Christian, that it may allow the sacred things to which it points to give a false sanctity to its institutions that are very human.

There is one assumption about the Church that must be

made quite clear at the outset. The Church should not be an exclusive sect made up of those who count themselves to be righteous or of those who hold the same opinions about controversial social questions. The Church should include any who recognize the claim of Christ upon them and who have the beginnings of faith in him as the supreme revelation of God or who seek to have the beginnings of faith in him. They may be weak and faltering and inconsistent and sinful. John Calvin was not easy-going in his attitude toward the Christian life but he quite rightly emphasized that only by the mercy of God could anyone be a member of the true Church. He said: "Nor does God only once receive and adopt us into his Church by the remission of sins; he likewise preserves and keeps us in it by the same mercy."[3] The Church is meant for people who need help.

It is inevitable that the Church will include people of different views concerning most public questions. Even if they were equally sincere and sensitive in forming opinions they would still differ because of the morally neutral factors in most social judgments. They would still differ because they would view the same problem from different positions in society; and even if the individual Christian is not in any crass way determined by economic interest it would still be natural for him to see with special clarity the valid elements in the side of a question that is in harmony with the interests of the people among whom he moves. I am speaking of the way things would be in an ideal Church. In the actual Church there are deep cleavages that are chiefly reflections of class bias and racial pride. This is a consequence of the fact that the Church is made up of

---

[3] *Institutes of the Christian Religion*, IV, 1, 20.

weak and sinful human beings. The hope is that these weak
and sinful human beings in the context of the Christian
Church can be brought to repentance.

One general American assumption seems at first sight to
cut across anything that we may say about the responsibility
of the Church for public life. I refer to the belief in the
separation of Church and state. The separation of Church
and state stands for very important truths but it is dangerous
as a dogma or as a slogan unless carefully defined. It is obvious that, if Christianity is a religion that is concerned with
history and if Christian ethics are relevant to the whole of
life, the spheres of Church and state overlap in important
ways. Both Church and state seek the welfare of the same
community. The members of the Church are also citizens
who participate in the life of the state and their citizenship
is a Christian vocation concerning which they receive guidance from the Church if the Church is not asleep. We should
keep the formula of separation of Church and state but I
urge that we make sure what it does stand for, and not allow
it to be a general source of inhibition against action by the
Church in society.

The separation of Church and state stands for at least two
very necessary things. The first is the freedom of the Church
from control by the state. The Anglican Church has a won-
derful system in which most of the high offices of the
Church are filled by the Prime Minister, not without con-
sultation with the leaders of the Church, who were pre-
viously appointed in the same way, but with the exercise of
his own discretion, and yet that Church is one of the most
prophetic of the great Churches of Christendom. But this is
an English mixture not made for export. In most situations

the freedom of the Church depends upon the legal separation between Church and state. The second reason for insisting on the separation of Church and state is that it is the only way of safeguarding the national community from the monopolistic position of a particular Church. The attempt of any Church to gain special privileges for itself from the state is a road that leads to the serious curtailment of religious liberty.

There can be no danger when the Church, after much free discussion, seeks to influence the state, so long as the Church limits itself to those issues concerning which it has competence, and so long as the whole procedure is open and above board. This is quite different from manipulations behind the scenes by ecclesiastics who are assumed to be able to deliver large blocks of votes. The Church should not by high pressure impose upon the whole community a policy that can only be defended on the basis of assumptions that are peculiar to itself. It is easy for the Protestant to see that the Roman Church has overstepped the mark in some states, where it has forced upon the whole community regulations that belong to its own Church discipline in regard to birth control and divorce. The Roman Catholic would doubtless retort that some Protestant denominations have done the same kind of things in their zeal for national Prohibition. That is partly true, but in the case of Prohibition it was also a contest between regions, and in some regions between the country and the city.

Before I consider constructively the role of the Church as the bearer of Christian ethics in society it is necessary for me to speak about one major obstacle within the Church itself to the effective discharging of its responsibility. It is the fact so often noticed that the Church in its own life reflects the divisions and conflicts of the world. Professor Richard Niebuhr some years ago wrote a book that should speak to the conscience of every churchman. He shows how denominationalism in America is only in small part a matter of essential theological differences. He summarizes his criticism in this passage:

"It [denominationalism] represents the accommodation of Christianity to the caste-system of human society. It carries over into the organization of the Christian principle of brotherhood the prides and prejudices, the privilege and prestige, as well as the humiliations and abasements, the injustices and inequalities of that specious order of high and low wherein men find the satisfaction of their craving for vainglory. The division of the churches closely follows the division of men into castes of national, racial and economic groups. It draws the color line in the church of God; it fosters the misunderstandings, the self-exaltations, the hatreds of jingoistic nationalism by continuing in the body of Christ the spurious differences of provincial loyalties; it seats the rich and the poor apart at the table of the Lord, where the fortunate may enjoy the bounty they have provided while the others feed upon the crusts their poverty affords." [4]

American Churches are racial Churches. This is often true of the denominations but it is almost always true of the local churches. On this matter there is no substantial difference between the north and the south. Quite apart from the direct working of race prejudice one can see reasons for this situation. It is often claimed that the minority race has a

---

[4] *The Social Sources of Denominationalism*, (Holt, 1929) p. 6.

better opportunity to develop its own leadership when it has
its own Churches. This can hardly be denied. Also, it is true
that the racial separation within the Church is often part of
a much larger problem of social and cultural congeniality
in the Church, a problem that is still present where there
are no racial differences. This larger problem is especially
acute for Protestantism, because both the sermon and the
Church supper are culturally and socially divisive. Protestant
Churches tend to be clubs held together by feelings of congeniality. Even some denominations have this characteristic.
These considerations indicate that we cannot deal with the
racial problem as an isolated problem but they make the
truth even more bitter. It is intolerable that the Church of
Christ should intensify these divisions. It is imperative that
the Church in the north and in the south find ways of overcoming racial segregation in its own life. It can say nothing
that carries conviction to the world until this scandal in the
Church has been removed.

It is also true that American Churches are class Churches.
If one takes American Protestantism as a whole in the north
and in the south one finds that it includes a cross section of
the population. But Protestant denominations are separated
in some cases by class lines. Local Churches tend to be class
Churches. In the industrial centers, especially in the north,
Protestantism has lost contact with the working class. The
lay leadership of the stronger denominations comes chiefly
from the comfortable middle classes. A report on the State
of the Church presented by a committee appointed by the
Federal Council of Churches in 1936 made a sharp criticism
of the Churches at this point. It said: "The leaders of the
local Protestant churches, particularly those which have the

largest influence, do not belong to the stratum of the American people (whose incomes are below $2000). They are likely to look and very often do look, with hesitation and fear upon the struggle of the masses for better conditions of life."

The results of this racial and social stratification within the Church are at present disastrous in their effect upon the ethical influence of the Church in the world. I shall summarize some of these results. There is first the obvious fact that the life of the Church belies its teaching. It teaches the equal dignity of all men before God, it teaches that the Christian life is a life of fellowship across all the barriers that separate men in the world, but its practices are very much like the practices of hotels.[5] A second result is that the Church is not at present in a position to be a very significant solvent of social conflict within the nation or within the local community. In the effort to discover the best application of Christian principles to controversial questions, the same Church does not have within it all the most important groups involved, and therefore the mutual correction of one another's judgment by different social perspectives in the light of the Gospel does not take place. This means in practice that the minister, if he is ethically sensitive, has the almost impossible task of representing to his own laymen the insights and the valid interests of those who are not themselves present in the congregation. A third result is that there is a tendency for two distorted kinds of religion to develop in Churches that are separated by a social chasm. Professor Liston Pope has shown how this can happen in

---

[5] I am not intending a special slur on hotels. A hotel is a piece of the world and makes no pretensions.

his study of the Churches in Gaston county, North Caro-
lina. He finds there what he calls the uptown churches—
those that are dominated by the business and professional
groups—and the mill churches where the mill workers worship. He notes the differences between these two kinds of
religion by saying, "If religion in the mill villages is largely
an escape from economic conditions, religion in the uptown
churches is to a considerable degree a sanction of prevailing
economic arrangements." [6] Both types of religion are per-
versions of Christianity and in that county studied by Professor Pope there seemed to be no leaders, ministers or laymen, who have sought to break either of those patterns. In
many other American counties there is prophetic leadership
in the Church that at least modifies the patterns of religious
escape or of moral complacency. But it is doubtful if any
Church can have a very stable hold upon the meaning of the
Christian faith for society unless the members of one class
have some contacts with the life of other classes within the
fellowship of the Church. [7]

I have dealt at some length with this great negative fact
about the life of the Church because it sets the Church one
of its major tasks. The Church must not wait until it has
success here before it does other things and even in spite of
this handicap there is much that can be achieved.

In what follows I shall deal with the ethical functions of
the Church in society under three general heads. The first is
the indirect influence of the Church in so far as it is true to

---

[6] *Millhands and Preachers*, (Yale, 1942) p. 92.

[7] I have dealt more fully with this and other obstacles before the Church
in a chapter in one of the volumes of *The Interseminary Series*, Vol. II,
entitled *The Gospel, the Church, and the World*, published by Harper &
Brothers in 1946. There are some echoes of this chapter in the above para-
graphs which its publishers kindly permit.

its commission. The second is direct social teaching within the Church but with the emphasis upon the action of the individual members in the world. The third is direct teaching and action by the Church in the world. Such an analysis as this, if it is thought to involve the separation of these functions from one another, is obviously artificial. But it may be helpful in enabling us to survey the field as a whole in a systematic fashion.

The indirect influence of the Church in public life can be seen in its contribution to the general moral tone of the community. It can be seen in the fact that there is still an impressive deposit of Christian moral convictions in most secular nations that have had a Christian background. The concern for social justice that is the most healthy element in Communism is rooted in the Hebrew-Christian tradition that was kept alive in the western world by the Church. The other most important ethical aspect of that tradition, the high value placed upon the individual person as a child of God, has had its influence in the liberal democratic institutions of the western world. The separation of these two ethical interests and the great distortion of each in the separation is calamitous.

There are two examples of the indirect influence of the Church to which I have referred in passing, but both should be mentioned here. One is the Church acting as a bond that unites men, in spite of particular conflicts between them. My discussion of the Church as reflecting the racial and the social divisions in the world should make it clear that any claims to be made for the Church at this point must be carefully limited. The ecclesiastical divisions in the Church have been sources of social conflict, and some of them continue to have that effect. But there is one area where we can point to the possibility that the Church may help men to bridge the chasms between them, and that is the area of international relations. In the years between the two world wars a profound change came over the Christian Church. There developed a greater degree of unity among Christians of all of the non-Roman branches of the Church than had existed in four centuries. The Church, as the result of the missionary movement, exists now in almost every country or region in the world. The hatreds of the war have not torn the Church apart. The second world war divided humanity more profoundly than the first world war, but the Church was held together better in the recent war than was the case in the earlier war. The ecumenical institutions, of which the World Council of Churches is the most important, have come out of the war with strength, and in the early post-war period there is evidence of the beginning of reconciliation between Christians who have been enemies. Such reconciliation began first between Christians in Germany and Christians in nations that were arrayed against her, but it was soon followed by the beginning of reconciliation between Christians in Japan and in America. In general the Church is far too much like the world, but in the attitude of Christians toward their national enemies there has been a different spirit than has been characteristic of the secular press and of public opinion outside the Church.

There have been striking examples of a sense of solidarity among the Christians of the world during the period of the war and its immediate aftermath. One example was the way in which Christians have tried to bear each other's burdens. The Churches of Britain which have suffered so much from the bombing have let it be known that they do not want a penny of aid from America for rebuilding because the continent needs help so much more grievously. Also the British have announced as their policy that ten percent of all that they raise for the rebuilding of their own Churches is to go to the Churches on the continent. Another example is the extraordinary demonstration of solidarity with the peoples of other lands that has come to characterize the missionary movement. It is often said in a scoffing way that missionaries have been the agents of western imperialism. Whatever truth there may have been in that in the past, the more common thing now is for missionaries to be the representatives to the western nations of the peoples among whom they work. They very often stand for the real welfare and just claims of the people of Japan. They have often become as Chinese as the Chinese in their identification of themselves with the people of that nation. They speak up for the rights of the people of Africa. They may at times become partisan and one-sided in their solidarity with the peoples whom they represent, but that is a good corrective for the exploitation or neglect that usually characterizes western attitudes toward those peoples.

In stressing this contribution of the Church toward the solidarity of the nations it should be admitted that there are divisions in the world that the Church is not at present in a position to do anything to overcome. A conflict between two non-Christian groups such as the Hindus and the Moslems in India is one example. But more fateful for the future of the whole world is the post-war tension between the Soviet Union and the western democracies. Here there is a tendency for the Church to increase the conflict, as in the case of the long-standing Roman Catholic crusade against Communism, and in the case of the bitterness between national branches of the Eastern Orthodox communion. Whether the Russian Orthodox Church will in the near future gain sufficient freedom from the Russian state to be a point of contact between Russia and the West is questionable. There are real grounds for conflict between Christians in the western democracies and Communism but Christians should not forget the responsibility of the Church in the past for allowing the spiritual chasm between itself and the movements of the left to develop and, whatever happens, they should not once more become a front for capitalistic or feudal opposition to Communism. How we can resist the spread of Russian totalitarianism and yet keep some perspective concerning our own past failures which have made Communism seem to many in the west to promise a better life; how we can oppose the Russian Church in so far as it is an instrument of the Russian state and yet hold the door open for cooperation with that Church in the ecumenical movement—these are problems for which I have no solution and I mention them in this context because to stress the contribution of the Church toward world unity without doing so would be less than candid.[8]

A second example of the indirect influence of the Church

---

[8] One can admit the subservience of the Russian Church to the state without being cynical about the new position of religion in Russia. There are some freedoms for the Church in its inner life both for worship and for education in the Christian tradition. If it makes the most of the freedom which it claims to have to circulate the Bible and to educate its own members, it has a chance to have some indirect influence upon the Russian community, and in some measure to interfere with the unity of Marxist culture. Criticism of state policy by the Church is out of the question for a long time, but light and power may come from Christian truth in unexpected ways.

upon social policy is the contribution that it makes to freedom. The existence of the Church as a community within
the larger community, as a community that does not owe
its existence to the state and that does not limit its loyalty
to the nation, but which in all of its worship and teaching
acknowledges the sovereignty of God, is a protection against
totalitarianism. The Church which has a gospel that it must
preach in order to be true to its very nature as a Church will
demand freedom to preach it and, if it is in any measure
successful, will hold the door open for the freedom of others
to criticize the state. This has been true on a large scale during the years of Nazi domination in Europe. Even where
there is no immediate threat to freedom it is of incalculable
importance to have within the nation this community with
a stable structure, with universal ties, and with a faith and a
commission which transcend the perspective of the nation.
It is true that an authoritarian Church that secures political
power or that is in alliance with an authoritarian state may
become a menace to freedom. In only a few countries is that
an immediate danger now, and even an authoritarian
Church, when it is a minority as the Roman Catholic Church
has been a minority in Germany, may help to safeguard the
freedom of others. A Church that is in its own life democratic and which encourages criticism of itself will be a resource for freedom at any time, and when tyranny threatens
it will be equipped to resist it both for itself and for others.

This indirect influence of the Church is never to be separated from the more direct teaching that I shall soon describe
for it becomes the more effective if that teaching is carried
on, but the heart of this indirect influence is an unintended
byproduct of Christian worship and of Christian fellowship.

It is often argued that the Church is not an end in itself but rather a means to another end, the Kingdom of God. As a protest against the kind of preoccupation with the institutions of the Church, into which it is easy for churchmen to drift, this argument has some merit. But worship in the Church is an end in itself, though it will lead to good practical results if it is sincere Christian worship. It is wrong to consider the actual fellowship that is realized in the Church to be only a means to world peace or to a similar social objective. It has its own meaning as a partial embodiment of the Kingdom of God. It is wrong to think of the life of faith within the Church only as a source of morale for work in the world. Through this life of faith the person becomes reconciled to God, to that which is for him life's center; it has its own justification and it meets needs that are deeper than those that can be met by social policies. To regard the Church as a means, in the sense of making these central aspects of its life subordinate to its influence on society, is to turn things around and gradually to undercut that influence. A Church that ceases to be God-centered, that does not mediate the distinctively Christian gospel, that does not meet the deeper levels of human need, that does not have an ultimate faith that transcends all success and failure of social policy— such a Church may be used for a time to promote this or that social cause but it will become secularized. The indirect social effects of what the Church is depend upon its vitality as a worshipping community.

I shall now turn to the second type of Church activity that has important ethical consequences—*direct social teaching within the Church with the emphasis upon the action of the individual members of the Church in the world.*

The Church can act in the world best through the work of its members in their various vocations and as citizens. If it cannot influence them it can hardly expect to influence the world outside the Church. If it can influence them, then much can be done to raise the level of public life. When I speak of the Church influencing its members a problem is immediately raised, because as a human community the Church itself is made up of its members. But the teaching of the Church is not what a majority of its members happen to think at a given moment. The Church exists as a response to a revelation of God's purpose in Christ and there is always the task of bringing the thinking of the members of the Church under the guidance and criticism of that revelation. It is the responsibility of the clergy to keep the ethical demand that is explicit or implicit in that revelation before the members of the contemporary Church. There are few things more objectionable in Church life than any form of clericalism that puts the clergy on a pedestal of their own, that keeps them a separate and closed group, that discourages the criticism of the clergy by the laity, or the sharing of power in the Church by the laity. But the clergy have an opportunity that most laymen do not have to become familiar with all the guidance that Christian teaching can bring from the past to the present, from the larger Church to the local Church. They have a function in this respect which they should gladly share with any laymen who can help them. At those points where Christian teaching must be related to concrete decisions the clergy can often learn from the laymen more than they can teach.

In the previous chapter much of this teaching was implied. I shall not go over that ground again except to mention a few of the most important elements that should come to be familiar as a matter of course to the people in a Christian Church.

The fact that Christianity is relevant to public life should be known. All the various distortions of the gospel that find in it only an other-worldly or only an individualistic message should be criticized. There is a vast amount of elementary teaching that is needed here in the Church School and in sermons.

The ethical norms by which every institution and every custom and every policy should be judged need to be taught in season and out of season so that people will have consciences that are instructed.

Existing institutions and practices should be criticized in the light of these norms. That will keep the general principles from being platitudinous. This quickly becomes dangerous ground but if it is avoided for that reason the Church fails at a point so central that no degree of piety and no theological profundity can compensate for the failure.

Even more difficult, the Church should help to reveal to its members their own motives, so that they will understand the extent to which they are controlled by narrow interests or by some form of group pride. Can the tendencies that give rise to the belief in economic determinism be deflected by Christian faith and Christian teaching? The answer would be "not fully" but a serious attempt has hardly been made to bring the respectable economic behavior of Christians under the discipline of an instructed Christian conscience. Quite essential is the habit of mind that begins with one's own shortcomings and those of one's own group. That is difficult but it is possible on the basis of Christian assump-

tions, and especially in the atmosphere of Christian worship.
Let it be a running commentary on the prayer of "general
confession."

The next element in this teaching inside the Church is the
presentation of what were called in the previous chapter
"middle axioms"—those goals that represent the demands
of Christian love upon our generation.

Last of all, there should be teaching about the responsibility of the individual to make his own decisions in regard
to the most difficult concrete problems that demand action.
These decisions usually involve controversy. They make it
necessary to take sides in a partisan political conflict. They
call for alliances with groups that do not share Christian
assumptions. They send the Christian soldier to battle when
there seems to be no other way to resist a tyrannical aggres-
sor. They send the Christian statesman to the legislature or
to an international conference to secure the best results he
can get from the attempt to compromise conflicting interests
and purposes. They send some out to take a lonely stand
that involves the renunciation of the compromises of ordinary political life in order that somewhere there may be a
clear witness to the ultimate Christian ideal. Here the Christian conscientious objector to war has a function. The
Church should prepare men in all these cases for the kind
of obstacles and set-backs that can be expected so that they
will not give up the struggle in disillusionment. There will
be needed a rekindling of faith in God's power that is
shown in the judgments which descend upon the attempts
of men to organize their world without reference to his
purpose, that is shown in the structures of order and justice
that do exist as the result of generations of conscientious

striving, and that is shown in the strange effectiveness that can be ascribed to the work of those who have become through their costly obedience instruments of God's love.

If the Church were to concentrate on this second phase of its work, and were to do nothing directly as a Church in the world, it might be enough. It would be moving the world through its members. But actually it can hardly go this far without going further. If it is measurably successful in changing the minds of its members in the ways I have suggested, they will demand various forms of direct action. They will want to organize as churchmen in order to influence public life more quickly. There are dangers in this, but if it were never attempted it would be a sign of indifference.

When we consider such *direct action* by the Church in the world we must take account of the warnings against it. Archbishop Temple, who was persistent and in the best sense radical in his emphasis upon the social implications of Christianity, was very decisive in his warning against corporate action on controversial public issues by the Church. He wrote: "It is of crucial importance that the Church acting corporately should not commit itself to any particular policy." The chief reason he gave for this was that "a policy always depends on technical decisions concerning the actual relations of cause and effect in the political and economic world; about these a Christian as such has no more reliable judgment than an atheist, except so far as he should be more immune to the temptations of self-interest." [9] In view of this situation Temple believed that we should not suggest that anyone who may differ from the majority of Christians on issues of this kind is any less a Christian on that account.

[9] *Christianity and Social Order*, (Penguin) p. 18.

Temple in his speeches and writings employed a very interesting device. He first outlined the distinctively Christian principles on a certain subject and then he advanced his own suggestions concerning the way in which these principles might be applied. He was careful to say that these suggestions were not necessary deductions from Christian principles and that he was offering them as illustrations to give substance to the principles. In one book he put these suggestions in regard to specific policies into an appendix. What actually happened was that people paid more attention to the daring suggestions toward a concrete program than to the principles, and because the Archbishop of Canterbury was their author they seemed to the world to come with impressive authority from the Church. There was quite an uproar, for example, when he modestly suggested that it might be a good thing to socialize the banks.

It is useful in attempting to form a judgment concerning how far the Church should go in taking a stand for or against a particular policy to distinguish between the various degrees of authoritativeness in corporate action by the Church. An analysis of these may clear our minds of much of the confusion on this subject. The most authoritative form of Church teaching and action in Protestantism is the incorporation of support of a specific policy into the creed or ethos of the Church. The ethos of Quakerism and of other so-called peace Churches includes pacifism. It would be difficult to point to many cases of this degree of identification with a particular policy. Perhaps support of Prohibition had a similar place in the ethos of Methodism and of several Protestant denominations. The next stage in authoritativeness would be the resolutions of the representative Church bodies such as the Presbyterian General Assembly or the Methodist General Conference. There are several other forms of action which rank below these but which are difficult to grade in relation to each other: the action of groups of ecclesiastical leaders, who cannot be dissociated from their Churches, the policies of such permanent agencies as Church Boards, the action of such a body as the Executive Committee of the Federal Council of Churches which in theory speaks for itself but which also appears to speak for the whole constituency to some extent. One agency that belongs in still another category somewhat below those mentioned in authority is an organization of Churchmen that uses the name of the Church but which is entirely unofficial. I refer to such an agency as the Methodist Federation for Social Service.

There has been developed a kind of Church teaching and action that is legally unofficial but which has considerable authority. The Church sometimes appoints a commission or a conference to speak for itself to the Church. What this group says or does may have enormous weight, but technically it speaks only for itself. The Conferences on a Just and Durable Peace in Delaware, Ohio, in 1942, and in Cleveland, in 1945, were in this category. The Federal Council during the recent war appointed a commission of theologians on "the Church and the war in the light of the Christian faith." This commission made two reports to the Federal Council dealing with central theological and ethical problems raised by the war, for which the members of the commission were alone responsible. The commission was officially created to report unofficially. Those who are now responsible for the policies of the World Council of Churches are exploring ways by which it can speak to the Churches words of guidance that can have intrinsic authority but which will not commit the constituent Churches.

There are two opposing views of this kind of procedure. There are those who fear it because they do not want to have even the most indirect association with statements with which they do not fully agree. They prefer to have the Church remain silent until it can speak officially with decisive authority. There are others, and I am one of them, who fear that if the Church is so restrained it will seldom say anything that is important until it is too late. What is needed is as much corporate Christian guidance as possible. The emphasis should be placed upon its intrinsic rather than its official authority, and freedom to oppose it must be taken for granted. Those who are responsible for such unofficial corporate guidance need to be fully aware of all the reasons for emphasizing the autonomy of technical judgments and the transcendence of Christianity. They should learn from previous mistakes, from wrong identifications of Christian faith and ethics with particular programs in the past. They should make it clear that on the issues concerning which there is no distinctively Christian wisdom they do not commit those who conscientiously disagree with their conclusions.

I shall now give three contemporary examples of teaching and action by the Church that will illustrate on various levels what I have said in abstract terms.

1. The Congregational-Christian denomination has a Council for Social Action that is appointed by the General Council of the Congregational-Christian Churches and is supported financially by the local Churches. This Council

has the right to speak for itself on social questions without consulting the General Council. It appoints several committees which have the right to speak for themselves without consulting the Council for Social Action. For example, it has a Legislative committee made up of members who live in the national capital and who in exercising this right to speak for themselves publish a monthly *Washington Report* in which they make recommendations to members of the Churches concerning specific legislation before Congress. Sometimes they are asked to represent the Council for Social Action or the General Council in testifying before Congressional committees on specific legislation, but that is a secondary function. More important is their function to suggest support of or opposition to specific legislation. At no point is the Church as a Church committed to specific legislation, but the opportunity for guidance for action from various agencies of the Church is always present.

2. A second illustration is taken from the experience of the Presbyterian Church (U.S.A.)—the northern branch of Presbyterianism. The Department of Social Education and Action appointed a committee in 1942 to study industrial relations. This committee consisted of representatives of management, Labor Unions and the clergy. It worked for two years on a report on "The Church and Industrial Relations." The Presbyterian Church for more than a generation has had an official position that was favorable to Labor Unions but here was a full statement on the subject which included emphasis upon the importance of Labor Unions both for the workers themselves and for American democracy, together with a frank account of the undesirable characteristics of some Unions, especially their lack of internal de-

mocracy. This report came very close to suggesting that Christians have a moral obligation to join a Labor Union. This was put in the following words: "We believe the Christian Church must confront its members who are employees with their obligation to consider their relation to a labor union in the light of the Christian principle of social responsibility. We believe industrial relations generally stand a stronger possibility of improvement when management and labor are organized. The good that follows upon such organization works for the benefit of those who assume neither the obligations nor the responsibilities of union membership, which gives the labor movement social value and ethical validity." That statement is typical of the report.

This report was adopted by the General Assembly of the Presbyterian Church (U.S.A.) in 1944 as its official position on these very difficult problems of industrial relations. But that was not all. The Presbyterian Board of National Missions was directed to set up several training schools for the clergy across the country to train ministers so that they can deal in an understanding way with industrial relations. A month's course, paid for by the denomination, on the basis of this report is made available to the ministers of the Presbyterian Church. The Presbyterian Church is conservative in habit. It draws its support from the comfortable middle classes to a greater extent than most other denominations, but here it is deliberately trying to correct its class bias, and it is taking an official position on issues that have great importance for the American public and which can arouse bitter controversy and conflict.

3. A third example of action by the Church is the mobilization of Christian opinion in favor of the San Francisco

Charter. I have already touched on this in an earlier chapter but I refer to it again as an illustration of one form of action by the Church. The Federal Council of Churches through its Commission on a Just and Durable Peace led the Protestant denominations in thinking about the problems of the peace.[10] Most of the denominations had their own parallel programs. The Churches saw America facing a great national decision. They knew that they were against isolationism and against imperialism. They knew in general what kind of world they wanted. They were puzzled to some extent about the San Francisco Charter, but except for a small minority they believed that the rejection of the Charter would be to take the wrong turn at that moment of fateful decision.

It is not my purpose to discuss the Charter here but to call attention to this general pattern of activity. I believe that it will often be the pattern for the Church. It will recognize the fatefulness of a particular decision. It will know with clarity what it is against. And it will necessarily find itself throwing its weight behind a policy that on the whole shows some promise of saving the nation or the world from taking the wrong turn. It should keep that policy under criticism, but its criticism should be so stated that it does not give aid and comfort to those who would seek to lead the nation in the opposite direction. Usually such action will be taken on issues that do not divide the political parties, though

---

[10] Mr. Henry R. Luce, who is in a favorable position to judge the influences that change public opinion, says of the improvements of the San Francisco Charter over the Dumbarton Oaks proposals: "In my observation, the greatest single influence at work in bringing about this salutary transformation was the Federal Council of Churches' Commission on a Just and Durable Peace." (From address by Mr. Luce on "The Ethical Problems Facing America," Duke University, February 12, 1946.)

when such a party arises as the National Socialist party in Germany the Church should oppose it.

These examples of activity by the Churches do not belong wholly to any one of the three general types of influence that the Churches should be expected to exercise on the world. In the main they illustrate direct action by the Church as a Church in regard to social policy. All three types of influence should be seen together. The point where concentration is needed is direct teaching on the meaning of Christian faith and ethics for social policy within the Church so that its members in their vocations and as citizens may be changed, actually converted, in conviction and purpose. In so far as our conviction and purpose are changed, the completely indirect influence of the Church which was first described will be greatly enhanced and it will be freed from some of the ambiguities that now cancel much of the good in it. The Christian, trained within the Christian Church, must make his own choices in the world, and the possibilities between which he must choose should have more promise because the Christian Church is in the world.

Note on Christian Ethics and the Ethics of Natural Law

ONE of the most controversial issues in contemporary Christian thought is the relation between the ethics based upon Christian revelation and the more general ethics of what is called "natural law," the moral law which men know by reason. This issue divides Barth and Brunner and in general it is discussed very differently among Protestant thinkers on the European continent and in Britain and America. In fact this controversy is so little noticed in American thought that I have not dealt with it except by inference in the main body of this book. The subject is approached with different presuppositions by Protestants and Catholics. In chapter III I have referred to the Catholic confidence that the human reason, apart from revelation, can know what the moral law is for society and have suggested some criticisms of it.

There are at least four reasons for the widespread doubt concerning the existence of a moral law of nature that can be known apart from revelation. One is the tendency in some theological circles, while stressing the claims of revelation, to encourage scepticism concerning the competence of human reason in the moral and religious sphere. Allied with this is a doctrine of man that assumes the corruption of reason as an essential aspect of the general sinfulness of man. A third reason for it is the secular moral relativism that casts doubt concerning the existence of universal moral standards, a relativism that is often taken by Christian thinkers to be a good preparation for faith in revelation. A fourth, and probably the most important reason in practice, is the fact that in Europe especially there has been a breakdown of all common moral assumptions. Anyone who has had first-hand experience of the chasm between the mentality of National Socialism and the moral convictions of the Christian and the humanistic West is naturally doubtful concerning the reliability of any universal rational morality. All four reasons have often been effective in the minds of the same persons.

Those who reject the morality of natural law seem to me to argue too often from the fact that cannot be denied that natural law is not universally known. Perhaps it is never known without distortion. But I do not see why this should be a ground for discrediting human reason in matters of morality, any more than the fact that faith in revelation is not universal should be a ground for discrediting faith. One difficulty is that when Christian thinkers make claims for this universal moral law they usually claim too much. Jacques Maritain, as a Roman Catholic, makes a significant admission when he says that while this law is written in the heart of man, it is "hidden from us as our own heart." He continues: "This metaphor itself has been responsible for a great deal of damage, causing natural law to be represented as a ready-made code rolled up within the conscience of each of us, which each one of us has only to unroll, and of which all men should naturally have an equal knowledge." [1] The critics of natural law are absolutely right in protesting against the belief that reason is proof against distortion and blindness.

The argument from the Bible and from Christian history is on the side of some recognition of a general revelation of the moral law. Paul's words about the law written in the heart (Romans 2:14-15) are difficult to explain away. Those who have least confidence in the morality of natural law make much of the Ten Commandments as revealed moral truth, but surely this revelation cannot be torn completely out of its historical relationship to moral codes outside the Bible. Neither Calvin nor Luther can be used as a supporting witness by those who take this negative position about the significance of natural law. Calvin, in spite of his dark view of fallen human nature, admitted that men had by nature the moral insight necessary for civil order. He assumes a universal acceptance of the laws necessary for society. He goes so far as to say in a carefully reasoned passage which deals with what men retain in spite of the fall that "not a person can be found who does not understand, that all associations of men ought to be governed by laws, or who does not conceive in his mind the principles of those laws." [2] That goes beyond the claim for natural law that I am making in these pages. There is ample evidence that Luther believed in the importance of natural law for the public order though here as elsewhere his thought is a

---

[1] *The Rights of Man and Natural Law,* (Scribners, 1943) p. 62.
[2] *Institutes of the Christian Religion,* Book II, ii, 13.

battleground for interpreters.[3] The historical argument is not conclusive because the Reformers, in common with Thomas Aquinas and the Schoolmen, had no such experience as we have had of the breakdown of the moral unity of western civilization. So long as common moral assumptions prevailed in the world that one knew it was natural to infer universal acceptance of the moral law.

Moreover it must be admitted by those who deny the significance of this moral law that it is necessary for Christians and non-Christians to cooperate on practical issues in society. Karl Barth called upon all men who were not corrupted by National Socialism to combine to resist Hitler. He asked Christians to do it on Christian grounds, but the overlapping of moral purpose that held together Christians, Jews, secular believers in freedom and democracy and Communists was and is a major reality in the contemporary world. Indeed the horror resulting from the denial of morality under the Nazis created such a revulsion that there has been in wide circles a fresh understanding of the importance of moral standards. I doubt if there were ever so many people as there are today who are deeply committed to inter-racial justice. This alliance may be split on the Communist issue in many countries but it will not be a clear division between Christians and non-Christians. Nor does Communism in-

---

[3] There is a careful discussion of the evidence concerning Luther's use of natural law in an article by John T. McNeill, "Natural Law in the Thought of Luther" in *Church History* (September, 1941). Professor McNeill returns to the subject in a later article, in which he makes this generalization: "with the possible exception of Zwingli they [the Reformers] all on occasion express a quite ungrudging respect for the moral law naturally implanted in the human heart, and seek to inculcate this attitude in their readers." (Article on "Natural Law in the Teaching of the Reformers" in *The Journal of Religion*, July, 1946.)

volve a complete break with the moral tradition of the West for, while Communists may often be morally cynical about immediate policies, they still envisage their ultimate goals in terms of justice and freedom and, more than they would admit, their teaching carries conviction because of its moral rather than its "scientific" criticism of Capitalistic society. I shall summarize the view of the relation between Christian ethics and natural law that underlies this book.

1. There is a moral order in the world that can be known with varying degrees of clarity apart from revelation.

2. The knowledge of this moral order is not as a matter of fact universal but it has a much broader basis than the Christian faith.

3. Some of the perceptions of moral truth doubtless depend upon the direct or indirect influence of Christianity, but when once they are seen they can be supported by facts of experience that can be known apart from Christian faith.

4. There is great contemporary support apart from Christian faith for the following moral convictions: that the human race is one in the sense that there are no permanently superior and inferior human groups, one in origin, one in essential nature, one in the fact that mutual relations of friendship do now cross all actual social barriers, one in fateful interdependence; that society should be open to free criticism from within; that men and nations should be true to their pledged word; that justice on the corrective side should be administered with impartiality and that on the side of the distribution of wealth it should be so administered as to promote equal opportunity for all children to develop their capacities. I have expressed these principles in cold, minimal terms but, taken together, they furnish an extensive moral

law that has a basis in experience which is independent of Christian faith. They can all be denied in theory and they are all in too large measure denied in practice, but men will be forced back to them whenever they try to organize life without reference to them. This is so clear in the case of the interdependence of men that it has become a moral commonplace.

The formula for justice that has been most often used in natural law teaching is that each man should receive his due. I have tried to suggest that the determination of what a man's due is should be arrived at without favoritism or discrimination, and that at least in the case of children the determination of what is their due should be governed by the principle of equality. If these two points are conceded the debate can continue as to how punishment should be related to the crime and how income should be distributed, and we are not likely to go very far wrong.

5. The vivid understanding of the claim and of the range of these moral principles, especially the realization that they are binding on oneself or one's own group, is immeasurably strengthened by the influence of Christian faith within a given culture. There is one point at which this can be seen most clearly. It is widely believed by those who are not poisoned by doctrines of racial superiority that all persons as persons have dignity and should be treated accordingly. This belief may not be a matter of reason; rather it is itself a faith that is broader than the Christian faith and wherever it exists it is something for which we should be profoundly thankful. Christians commit a great wrong if they are supercilious toward this belief when it is mixed with what seem to them to be illusions about natural human goodness, about

the common man, and the like. But it is true—and here we come up against the difference between Christianity and Communism again—that this conviction concerning the dignity of all men will in most circles break down in relation to particular groups. It may appear to be a temporary breakdown that is different from crude ideas of race but it will be a breakdown none-the-less. It may be that some group will forfeit its claim to human dignity because it has become wrong politically—Kulaks or Fascists—or it may be that some group becomes for a while enemies of "our side" in war. The redemptive Christian concern for the lost sheep, for the sinner, for the enemy or opponent, for the marginal person who does not count as far as the world is concerned and who is yet a child of God, is the one clear safeguard of this moral principle of the unity of the human race against its being at least temporarily obscured even among "the righteous."

6. The principles of the moral law that I have described do not carry with them clear guidance concerning their application to concrete circumstances. When we come into the maze of means and ends, they settle few questions for us. If, for example, we are attempting to arrive at more immediate principles to determine what a "just wage" or income would be, we find ourselves forced to weigh such incommensurable considerations as actual contribution to production, personal or family needs, the effect of income upon incentive, the indirect effect of equality or inequality of living standards upon the health of society. All those factors must be weighed before we can determine what a just wage or income would be and no one can say that a particular conclusion on the subject would be valid for all situa-

tions. We must be on our guard against the common tendency to assume that methods and institutions which have general acceptance in one's own culture have the universal claim that truly belongs to the moral principles which they are designed to implement.

If we do not claim too much for it, we can defend the belief that there is a moral law that is known in part outside the orbit of Christian faith, that if known by those whose minds are formed by Christian faith it can be supported by facts of experience that they perceive together with men who do not share their faith. We should be clear about one thing —that those who call themselves Christians will often need to learn about the moral conditions for the good life and the good society from those who do not accept the Christian name. It is obvious that Christians and Jews share to an important extent the same revelation. Criticism and protest from outside Christian circles have often been a needed corrective for Christians. The radical movements for economic justice, the democratic protests against social hierarchies, the scientific concern for intellectual integrity, the belief in tolerance that stems from the Enlightenment have all been bearers of moral values to which Christians have been blind only too often, though these values have roots in the Christian tradition.

Within the full context of Christian faith the moral law comes into its own, and there are resources in Christianity which should prevent application of it in one-sided and distorted ways. Without the sensitivity and the power that are the fruit of faith and love, men fall far short even of the more general moral law. It is a mistake to believe in the existence of a self-sufficient reason that always knows the good, but it is also a mistake to deny that Christian moral conviction overlaps with a broader knowledge of the moral order that confronts Christians and non-Christians alike, and which, if they fail to heed it, will bring upon both a common impoverishment of life or a common destruction.

Index

Index

Althaus, Paul, 53
Ambiguity, moral, 17-28, 40, 47
  60
Anabaptists, 41
Anarchy, 7, 78
Anglican Church, 93
Apocalypse, 54
Aquinas, Thomas, 35n, 119
Aristotle, 40
Asceticism, 47; vocational, 33–34;
  sectarian, 41
Atomic war, 12, 20, 27–28, 39,
  48, 68
"Atomic Warfare and the Chris-
  tian Faith," 28n
Augustine, 16, 90

Baillie, John, 18
Bainton, R. H., 49
Barth, Karl, 12, 13n, 39, 55–56,
  85, 116, 119; Barthianism, 12
Berdyaev, Nicolas, 13n
Berlin, 20
Bible, Biblical, 11, 13, 39, 102n,
  118
Birth control, 94
Boland, F. J., 36
Bombing, obliteration, 20, 48, 72–
  73 (See also *Atomic war*)
Britain, 1, 4, 17, 56, 101, 116
British Council of Churches, 28n
British Labor Party, 38
Brunner, Emil, 13n, 25, 60, 86,
  116
Buchenwald, 12

Calvin, John, 6, 92, 118; Calvin-
  ism, 6, 52
Canada, 38
Capitalism, 13, 35, 42, 50, 102,
  120
Catholicism, 32–41, 52, 60, 116;
  Anglo–, 33; Roman, 1, 9, 32–
  41, 47, 68, 83, 94, 102, 103, 117;
  theology of, 34
Catholic Principles of Politics,
  36n
Children, 3–4, 80, 120, 121
*Children of Light and the
  Children of Darkness, The,*
  85n
China, 20, 30, 101
Christ, 91, 92, 95, 96, 105 (See
  also *Jesus*)
Christendom, 33n
Christian Civilization, Society, or
  State, 18–19, 33n, 34, 35, 37, 40,
  60, 89–90
Christian Faith, 18–19, 40, 60–61,
  62, 70, 73, 76, 77, 79, 90, 91,
  103, 104, 106, 110, 117, 120,
  121, 122
Christian News-Letter, The,
  56n
Christianity and Social Order,
  5n, 108n
Christianity and Society, 51n
Christianity and the Social Crisis,
  9n
Christianizing the Social Order,
  89n